1.1   Understanding the Digital Marketing Landscape 1

Navigating the Maze of Possibilities 1

The Digital Ecosystem: Where the Journey Begins 1

Embracing Diversity: Channels at your Disposal...1

The User's Journey: Guiding the Way 1

Data: The North Star of your Strategy..2

The Art of Storytelling: Crafting compelling narratives 2

The Ever-Changing Algorithmic Dance 2

The Power of Collaboration: Building Alliances 2

The Beginner's Mindset: Starting Strong 3

Conclusion: Navigating the uncharted Waters 3

Weaving Threads of Success 3

The Puzzle of Consistency: Crafting a unified Brand Identity...3

Audience-Centric Strategy: Meeting Users where they are. 3

The Amplification Effect: Reinforcing your Message. 4

The SEO and PPC Tango: Maximizing Visibility..4

Synchronization of Content: A storytelling Odyssey 4

Data-Driven Decisions: Insights across the Board 4

Cultivating Customer Relationships: Long-Term Engagement 5

Adaptability in a shifting Landscape: Future-Proofing your Strategy..............................5

Conclusion: The Symphony of Success..5

1.3   Synergy of PPC, SEO, and Social Media Marketing..5

Crafting a Seamless User Journey 5

Understanding the Triad of Influence..6

A Perfect User Journey...6

Conclusion: A synchronized Symphony of Success 7

The Pillars of Digital Marketing 9

2.1   PPC (Pay-Per-Click) Advertising - Navigating Google Ads and Microsoft Advertising 9

Understanding Google Ads and Microsoft Advertising 9

Benefits of PPC Advertising...10

Challenges of PPC Advertising 10

Performance Max Campaign and the AI Revolution 11

AI and Machine Learning: Pioneering the Future of PPC..11

Conclusion: Navigating the PPC Landscape with Foresight..11

2.2   **Unleashing the Power of PPC Advertising includes Paid Social** 12

Instant Visibility: Lighting Up the Digital Sky 12

Targeting Precision: The Bullseye Approach..13

The Power Couple: Instant Visibility and Targeting Precision 13

Conclusion: A Dual-Edged Sword of Success 13

Navigating Ad Blockers and Mitigating Risks in PPC Advertising.............................14

The Risks: Navigating choppy Waters 14

Mitigating Risks and Seizing Opportunities...15

Conclusion: Navigating Ad Blockers with Innovation and Adaptability 15

2.4   **The Rise of Search Generative Experience**...16

Transforming PPC Strategies, Challenges, and Advantages 16

Understanding Search Generative Experience 16

Challenges for PPC Marketers...16

Benefits for PPC Marketers 17

Adapting PPC Strategies for the Search Generative Experience..................................17

Conclusion: Embracing the Evolution with Foresight 18

2.5   **SEO (Search Engine Optimization)**...18

Unveiling SEO's Potential in a World of Generative Search: Navigating the Landscape of Evolving
User Interactions 18

The Dynamics of Generative Search 19

Unveiling SEO's Potential..19

Challenges and Opportunities..20

Conclusion: Pioneering SEO in the Generative Search Era 21

The Intricacies of Organic Reach 21

Navigating the Seas of Long-Term Credibility 21

The Power of Organic Reach in Generative Search 22

Contextual Resonance 22

Depth and Comprehensive Information...22

Forging Long-Term Credibility in the Generative Era 22

Conclusion: Navigating the Nexus of Reach and Credibility 23

2.7   **Navigating the Depths of Search Engine Algorithm Shifts: Adapting SEO Strategies in the
Age of Generative Search**..24

The Unpredictable Symphony of Algorithm Shifts..24

Adapting to Algorithmic Nuances 24

Strategies to Navigate Algorithm Shifts 24

Mitigating Algorithmic Risks 24

Capitalizing on Algorithmic Opportunities 25

Conclusion: Sailing Through Algorithmic Seas with Expertise 26

2.8   Post-Pandemic Search Behavior...26

Unveiling the Evolution of Post-Pandemic Search Behavior: Crafting SEO Strategies for a
Transformed Digital Landscape 26

A New Dawn of Search Behavior 26

Understanding the Evolution 26

Strategies for the Transformed Landscape 27

Mitigating Search Behavior Challenges 27

Harnessing Search Behavior Opportunities..28

Conclusion: Steering SEO Strategies with Insight 28

Harnessing Social Media's Impact 28

Understanding Social Media's Role 28

The Power of Storytelling and Engagement 29

Community Building and Customer Support 29

Driving Conversions and Sales...29

Leveraging Data for Precision 30

Navigating Challenges and Adapting 30

Seizing Opportunities and Staying Innovative 30

Conclusion: Unleashing the Potential of Social Media Mastery 31

Illuminating the Path to Building Lasting Brand Awareness and Loyalty: A Comprehensive Dive into
Strategies for Meaningful Impact 31

Understanding the Essence of Brand Awareness 31

Crafting Strategies for Sustained Loyalty...32

Empowering Emotional Connections 32

Effective Engagement Strategies...32

Fostering Advocacy and User-Generated Content (UGC) 32

Precision in Loyalty Measurement 33

Staying Adaptive and Evolving...33

Conclusion: Forging a Legacy of Brand Excellence 33

Decoding the Values and Behavior of Generation Z: A Profound Exploration into Connecting with the
Heart of the Future..34

Behavioral Patterns that Shape Gen Z Engagement 34

Connecting through Gen Z's Lens...35

Embracing Diversity and Inclusivity 35

Transparency and Ethical Practices 35

Adapting to Gen Z's Values 36

Conclusion: Pioneering Authentic Connections with Gen Z 36

2.12   Embracing Authenticity and Engaging Content..36

A Profound Exploration with Exemplary Brands..36

Creating Engaging Content that Resonates 37

Exemplary Brands Embracing Authenticity..37

Humanizing Through Empathy 37

Transparency as the Foundation 38

Creating Engaging Narratives..38

Conclusion: Forging a Legacy of Authenticity and Engagement Mastery 38

Chapter 3 39

Cutting-Edge Innovations and Trends 39

3.1   Google Lens: Revolutionizing Visual Search..39

Unveiling the Power of Google Lens: Navigating Benefits and Challenges for Marketers with
Exemplary Brand Implementations 39

The Marvel of Google Lens...39

Benefits for Marketers 40

Exemplary Brand Implementations 40

Navigating Challenges for Marketers..40

Seizing Opportunities with Google Lens...41

Conclusion: Pioneering a Visual Frontier with Google Lens Mastery 41

Mastering the Integration of Google Lens into Marketing Strategies: Elevating User Experiences with
Exemplary Brand Success Stories 41

Strategies for Seamless Integration 42

Benefits of Google Lens Integration..42

Exemplary Brand Success Stories 42

Overcoming Challenges...43

Creating Compelling Campaigns...43

Conclusion: Forging a New Era of Visual Engagement with Google Lens Mastery....................43

Unveiling the Nexus of Challenges and Benefits: Elevating User Engagement through Visual Content
Mastery 44

Navigating the Terrain of Challenges...44

Beneath the Surface of Benefits 44

Addressing Challenges with Strategic Approaches..45

Leveraging Benefits for Engaging Content 45

Exemplifying Success..46

Navigating Benefits with Wisdom..46

Conclusion: Pioneering Visual Content Excellence for Enduring Engagement 46

3.4   Search Generative Experience and MUM **47**

The Emergence of Search Generative Experience 47

The Essence of Search Generative Experience 47

Unified Convergence of Digital Marketing Channels 47

Importance of Holistic Collaboration 47

User Benefits and Empowerment **48**

The Embryonic State and Future Promise **48**

Exemplifying the Current Landscape **48**

Navigating Forward: A Unified Digital Odyssey **49**

Mastering MUM: Multilingual and Multimodal Approach **49**

Decoding MUM's Essence **49**

Elevating Engagement through Multimodal Power **49**

Impact on Global Accessibility **50**

Creating Multilingual and Multimodal Strategies **50**

Exemplary Brand Success Stories **50**

Crafting a Future-Proof Strategy **51**

Personalized User Experiences **51**

Innovating on the Horizon **51**

Conclusion: Forging a Global Legacy with MUM Mastery **51**

Challenges on the Content Horizon **52**

Embracing the Potential of Next-Gen Search **52**

Tailoring Content Strategies **52**

Exemplifying Content Brilliance **53**

Enriching User Engagement **53**

Navigating the Frontier: Challenges as Opportunities....................................**53**

Future-Proofing Content Creation **54**

Conclusion: Pioneering Next-Gen Content Excellence **54**

Chapter 4 ....**55**

Challenges on the Horizon for SEOs **55**

4.1   E-E-A-T (Experience, Expertise, Authoritativeness, Trustworthiness)...................**55**

What does E-E-A-T mean?...**55**

What are the challenges of E-E-A-T?...**56**

How important is E-E-A-T for websites and online shops? **56**

How to improve E-E-A-T for your website or online shop? **57**

Unpacking E-E-A-T's Significance..**58**

So, how can you improve your website's E-E-A-T?..**58**

Establishing Brand Authority and Trust: Forging Trust and Authority through E-E-A-T 5ξ

Building Brand Authority 5ξ

Establishing Trust 6C

Exemplifying E-E-A-T in Action 6C

Navigating Challenges and Opportunities 6C

Crafting an E-E-A-T Focused Strategy 6C

Future of E-E-A-T 61

Conclusion: E-E-A-T as the Cornerstone of Brand Eminence 61

4.2   Aligning E-E-A-T with SEO Practices: Forging a Symbiotic Union 61

Mechanics of E-E-A-T and SEO Synergy 62

Strategies for Seamless Integration 62

E-E-A-T's Impact on Page Ranking 63

Exemplifying E-E-A-T and SEO Success 63

Futureproofing with E-E-A-T and SEO 63

Conclusion: Orchestrating E-E-A-T and SEO Harmony for Unparalleled Impact 64

4.3   Future SEO Challenges and Solutions 64

Navigating Evolving Search Algorithms: Unveiling Solutions for a Dynamic Digital Landscape 64

Solution 1: Embrace User-Centricity and Quality 64

Solution 2: Strategic Data-Driven Insights 65

Solution 3: Technical Optimization Mastery 65

Solution 4: Adaptive SEO Techniques 65

Solution 5: Amplify User Engagement 65

Solution 6: AI-Enhanced Optimization 66

Solution 7: Holistic Brand Reputation Management 66

Solution 8: Cultivate Adaptive Agility 66

Conclusion: Mastering Algorithmic Evolution with Strategic Solutions 67

4.4   Mobile-First and Voice Search Optimization 67

Unveiling the Mobile-First and Voice Search Revolution 67

Mobile-First Optimization: Challenges and Strategies 67

Unlocking Mobile-First Possibilities 68

Voice Search Optimization: Challenges and Strategies 68

Embracing Voice Search's Potential 68

Seamless Integration of Mobile-First and Voice Optimization 68

Innovative Solutions for Accessibility 6ξ

Personalized Experiences and User Behavior 6ξ

The Future of Mobile-First and Voice Optimization 6ξ

Conclusion: Forging Ahead in the Mobile-First and Voice Search Epoch 70

Safeguarding Trust: Data Privacy and Ethical SEO Practices in the Digital Landscape 70

Data Privacy Challenges and Strategies 70

Upholding Data Privacy Possibilities 71

Ethical SEO Practices: Challenges and Strategies..71

Fostering Ethical SEO Excellence..71

Synthesis of Data Privacy and Ethical SEO 71

Striking the Balance for User Trust..72

Ethical SEO's Future Horizons 72

Conclusion: Forging Ethical Eminence in a Data- Driven Era 72

Chapter 5..73

Multimedia's Dominance in Digital Marketing 73

5.1   Embracing the Multifaceted Canvas: Multimedia's Dominance in Digital Marketing 73

5.2   Power of Video Content...74

The Cinematic Revolution: Unveiling the Profound Power of Video Content 74

The Ascendance of Video...74

Unraveling Video's Importance 74

Future Foresight: Why Videos Are Essential 75

Multichannel Strategy: The Art of Video Integration 75

Video SEO Mastery 75

Interactive Videos: Engaging the Viewer...76

Embracing Live Streaming: Real-Time Connection 76

User-Generated Content and Video..76

The Power of Emotional Appeal 76

Conclusion: Crafting a Video Symphony Across Channels 77

The Unstoppable Ascension: Chronicles of the Rise of Video Content Consumption 77

The Genesis: Birth of a Visual Revolution...77

The YouTube Revolution: A Catalyst for Change 78

The Mobile Era: A Game-Changer for Accessibility..78

Visual Storytelling: Eliciting Emotions and Connections...78

Social Media: The Power of Virality and Sharing..78

Live Streaming: Authenticity in Real-Time 78

Video-First Platforms: The Dawn of a New Era 78

Educational Renaissance: Learning Through Videos..78

The Future Envisioned: Video as the Lingua Franca 79

Conclusion: The Odyssey Continues: The Tapestry of Video Content Consumption 79

5.4   Tapping into Emotional and Visual Appeal: Navigating Challenges, Unveiling Possibilities
Challenges: Unveiling the Landscape of Emotion and Visuals...79

Possibilities: Crafting Compelling Emotional Narratives 80

Challenges: Harnessing Visual Appeal's Potential 80

Possibilities: Crafting Visually Arresting Content 80

Challenges: Balancing Emotional Depth and Visual Aesthetics..80

Possibilities: Crafting the Perfect Synthesis 81

Challenges: Measuring Emotional Impact and Visual Resonance 81

Possibilities: Analyzing Emotional and Visual Metrics 81

Conclusion: Mastering the Art of Emotion and Visuals 82

5.5   Crafting a Comprehensive Strategy 82

Navigating the Labyrinth of Digital Marketing Mastery...82

Foundation: Aligning with Business Objectives 82

Embrace the Digital Ecosystem..83

Content Creation and Distribution...83

Data-Driven Decision Making...83

Personalization for Engagement..83

Search Engine Optimization (SEO) Mastery..84

Social Media Amplification...84

Paid Advertising Precision 84

Email Marketing Excellence...85

Conversion Rate Optimization (CRO)...85

Innovative Technology Integration..85

Conclusion: Orchestrating a Masterpiece of Strategy 85

5.6   The Unified Approach to Digital Marketing: Weaving Threads of Excellence into a Singular
Strategy 86

Foundation: The Core Tenets of Unity..86

Synergy Across Channels 86

Content Harmonization...87

Data-Driven Insights...87

Personalization Across Channels...87

Paid and Organic Symbiosis 87

Unified Brand Voice...88

Customer-Centric Engagement..88

Innovative Technology Integration..88

Conclusion: Crafting a Singular Symphony of Success 88

The Symbiotic Dance: Unveiling the Synergy of PPC, SEO, Social Media, and Visual Content 89

Foundation: Orchestrating a Unified Vision 89

PPC, SEO, and Social Media: The Harmonious Trio 89

Visual Content: The Visual Thread 90

The User Journey: A Unified Odyssey 90

Keyword Synergy 91

Amplifying Social Media Engagement 91

Unified Analytics: Data-Driven Insights 91

Conclusion: Crafting a Symphony of Digital Mastery 91

5.8   Delivering Consistent Brand Message 92

Unveiling the Art of Consistency: Delivering a Brand Message That Resonates 92

Foundation: The Core of Cohesion 92

Strategies for Consistency 92

Omnipresence Across Channels 93

Email Communication Mastery 93

Visual Identity Reinforcement 93

Storytelling Continuity 93

Cross-Channel Synergy 94

Employee Advocacy: Amplifying the Echo 94

Feedback Loop for Refinement 94

Conclusion: The Symphony of Brand Resonance 95

5.9   Embracing Evolution 95

Agile Adaptation 95

Technology Integration 95

Human-Centric Focus 96

Sustainable Engagement 96

Embracing New Platforms 96

Staying Ahead of Search Evolution 97

Investing in Education 97

Conclusion: Crafting a Visionary Path Forward 97

5.10   Embracing Continuous Adaptation 97

Navigating the Winds of Change 98

Agility in Action 98

Integrating Cutting-Edge Technologies 98

Human-Centric Resonance 98

Sustainability and Ethical Practices 99

Embracing Emerging Platforms 99

Investing in Knowledge...99

Conclusion: Pioneering the Future Landscape...100

The Canvas of Creativity...100

Cultivating an Innovative Ecosystem 100

Nurturing a Creative Mindset 101

Inspiration in Data 101

Collaborative Creativity...101

The Role of Playfulness...102

Feedback Loop for Growth..102

Technology as a Muse 102

Conclusion: Sculpting a Masterpiece of Innovation..102

Embracing the Currents of Change..103

Strategic Evolution 103

Personalized Engagement..104

Innovative Storytelling 104

Cultivating User-Centricity 104

Cross-Channel Resonance 104

Innovating Ahead of the Curve..105

Conclusion: Forging a Resilient Legacy 105

5.13   The Future of Digital Marketing: Unifying Channels for Branding Success.......................105

Digital Marketing's Future Significance 106

The Power of Unified Channels 106

A Visionary Approach to Branding..106

Navigating the Uncharted Seas..106

Conclusion: Pioneering a Future of Brand Resonance 107

Closing words..107

Glossary 109

1.1 Understanding the Digital Marketing Landscape

Navigating the Maze of Possibilities

As we step into the dynamic realm of digital marketing, it's essential to grasp the multifaceted landscape that awaits us. Whether you're a beginner taking your first steps or an expert seeking to refine your approach, this chapter will serve as your compass through the ever-evolving world of digital marketing.

The Digital Ecosystem: Where the Journey Begins

Imagine the digital landscape as an expansive ecosystem teeming with opportunities and challenges. At its core are the platforms, channels, and tools that enable you to connect with your audience. From social media giants like LinkedIn, Tik Tok, Facebook and Instagram to search engine titans like Google and Bing, these platforms form the bedrock of your marketing efforts. Each has its own nuances, user behaviors, and algorithms that determine your success.

Embracing Diversity: Channels at your Disposal

Digital marketing isn't a one-size-fits-all solution. Instead, it's a symphony of channels, each with its distinct melody. Pay-Per-Click (PPC) advertising catapults your content to the top of search results and social feeds through strategic bidding. Search Engine Optimization (SEO) harnesses keywords and technical finesse to secure prime real estate on search engine result pages. Social Media Marketing dances with storytelling, hashtags, and community engagement. Email marketing, content marketing, influencer collaborations, and more - these are all instruments in your digital orchestra.

The User's Journey: Guiding the Way

Picture your potential customers as explorers navigating an intricate labyrinth. Your role as a digital marketer is to illuminate their path, making it easy for them to find your brand amidst the noise. Begin by understanding the stages of their journey: awareness, consideration, decision, and advocacy. At each stage, your strategy must evolve, providing the right information, emotions, and incentives.

Data: The North Star of your Strategy

In this data-driven age, insights reign supreme. Analytical tools empower you to demystify user behavior, track conversions, and measure the impact of your efforts. Google Analytics, Facebook Insights, and other platforms give you a backstage pass to understand what's resonating and what's not. This data guides your decisions, enabling you to optimize campaigns, pivot strategies, and align with your audience's preferences.

The Art of Storytelling: Crafting compelling narratives

At the heart of every successful digital campaign lies the art of storytelling. Your brand isn't just a product or service; it's a narrative waiting to be shared. The magic happens when you weave emotions, values, and solutions into your content. Relatability is the key; your audience should see themselves in your stories. Authenticity is the thread that weaves your brand into their lives.

The Ever-Changing Algorithmic Dance

As an experienced digital marketing manager, you're aware that the digital landscape is akin to a constantly shifting dance floor. Algorithms change, rules evolve, and trends emerge. What worked yesterday might not work today. Flexibility and adaptability are your allies. Stay attuned to industry news, attend webinars, and engage in continuous learning to stay ahead of the curve. Follow the right people on X & LinkedIn to be always up to date.

The Power of Collaboration: Building Alliances

In this labyrinth, you're not alone. Collaboration holds immense potential. Partner with influencers whose audiences align with your brand. Engage with your community through user-generated content. Collaborative efforts extend your reach, infuse fresh perspectives, and foster trust.

The Beginner's Mindset: Starting Strong

For beginners, the digital marketing landscape might seem overwhelming. Take a deep breath and embrace the journey. Start small, experiment, and learn from both successes and failures. Your journey is an expedition of discovery, and every step, no matter how small, brings you closer to mastering the art of digital marketing.

Conclusion: Navigating the uncharted Waters

Understanding the digital marketing landscape is akin to embarking on a grand adventure. It's a mix of creativity, data analysis, psychology, and technology. Whether you're just beginning or have sailed these waters for years, remember that the landscape is ever evolving. Embrace change, keep your finger on the pulse of innovation, and always strive to create meaningful connections with your audience. With this understanding, you're poised to navigate the digital maze and create marketing experiences that leave a lasting impact.

1.1   Importance of a Holistic Approach

Weaving Threads of Success

In the dynamic world of digital marketing, the concept of a holistic approach is not just a strategy; it's a philosophy that underscores the interconnectedness of all moving parts. As an experienced digital marketing manager, you recognize that the power of your efforts lies not in isolated actions, but in the orchestration of a synchronized symphony. In this chapter, we delve into why embracing a holistic approach is your ultimate key to unlocking unparalleled success.

The Puzzle of Consistency: Crafting a unified Brand Identity

Picture your brand as a puzzle, where every piece represents an element of your digital presence. A holistic approach ensures that each piece fits seamlessly, creating a cohesive and recognizable brand identity. From your website to your social media profiles, the tone, visuals, and values should align like pieces of a larger mosaic. Consistency breeds familiarity, and familiarity breeds' trust.

Audience-Centric Strategy: Meeting Users where they are.

One of the cornerstones of a holistic approach is understanding that your audience doesn't interact with your brand in isolation. They move fluidly across platforms, seeking information, entertainment, and solutions. By adopting a holistic mindset, you can meet them at various touchpoints, tailoring your content to suit their preferences and behaviors. A consistent experience regardless of the channel builds a sense of reliability.

The Amplification Effect: Reinforcing your Message.

Imagine each marketing channel as a thread in a tapestry. A single thread, no matter how vibrant, can only do so much. When woven together, they amplify the impact of your message. A holistic approach involves strategic amplification, where your message is harmoniously echoed across different channels. A social media post can link back to a blog, which in turn references a video. This interconnectedness enhances your brand's visibility and reinforces the core narrative.

The SEO and PPC Tango: Maximizing Visibility

In the dance of digital marketing, SEO and PPC are partners that complement each other. While SEO lays the foundation for organic visibility, PPC steps in to provide an immediate boost. A holistic strategy integrates both, ensuring that your brand occupies prime real estate on search engines. The result? A dynamic duo that drives traffic and conversions.

Synchronization of Content: A storytelling Odyssey

Content is the heart and soul of digital marketing. A holistic approach involves crafting content that transcends individual campaigns. Instead, each piece becomes a chapter in a larger story. Your blog posts feed into your social media campaigns, which in turn fuel your email marketing efforts. This synchronicity paints a vivid narrative that resonates with your audience at every stage of their journey.

Data-Driven Decisions: Insights across the Board

One of the most potent advantages of a holistic approach is the accessibility to comprehensive data. By analyzing data from various channels, you gain insights into how your audience behaves, which strategies yield the best results, and where adjustments are needed. These insights, when shared across channels, foster a culture of continuous improvement. Before you make relevant optimizing decisions, analyze all data you have: SEO data, PPC data, social media data - you need access to all platforms. Bring all the data together Power BI or looker studio - what you prefer.

Cultivating Customer Relationships: Long-Term Engagement

A holistic approach goes beyond transactional interactions. It nurtures re-lationships with your customers, transforming them into brand advocates. By engaging with them consistently across channels, you're not just selling products; you're offering a holistic experience. Whether they encounter your brand on social media, through email campaigns, or during their online searches, the sense of connection remains constant.

Adaptability in a shifting Landscape: Future-Proofing your Strategy

Digital marketing is in a perpetual state of evolution. New platforms emerge, algorithms change, and user behaviors shift. A holistic approach equips you with the adaptability to pivot without losing momentum. You're not reliant on a single channel; instead, you can adjust your strategy to accommodate the changing tides of the digital landscape.

Conclusion: The Symphony of Success

In a world where individual channels can feel like isolated notes, a holistic approach creates a symphony that resonates deeply with your audience. By weaving threads of consistency, synchronicity, and engagement, you transform your brand into an immersive experience that leaves an indelible mark. Whether you're engaging beginners or fellow experts, remember that the whole is truly greater than the sum of its parts. It's not just digital marketing; it's digital orchestration.

1.2 Synergy of PPC, SEO, and Social Media Marketing

Crafting a Seamless User Journey

In the realm of digital marketing, achieving success doesn't rest solely on the shoulders of individual strategies. Instead, it's the intricate dance of PPC, SEO, and social media marketing that creates a harmonious symphony capable of resonating with your audience on multiple levels. As an experienced digital marketing manager, you understand that the real magic happens when these forces unite to craft a seamless user journey.

Understanding the Triad of Influence

Pay-Per-Click (PPC)

PPC campaigns are like spotlight moments that instantly thrust your brand into the limelight. Through targeted ads, you ensure your message reaches the right people at the right time. Whether it's on search engines or social media platforms, PPC provides an immediate boost to visibility and can be precisely tailored to specific demographics.

Search Engine Optimization (SEO)

On the other side of the spectrum lies the slow-burning, evergreen power of SEO. It's the art of optimizing your website to organically climb search engine ranks. Through strategic keyword placement, technical finesse, and valuable content, SEO ensures your brand remains a steady presence in the digital landscape.

Social Media Marketing

Social media is the realm of connection and engagement. It's where you forge relationships, tell stories, and create a sense of community around your brand. Each post, comment, and share contribute to building brand loyalty and spreading your message through the digital word of mouth.

A Perfect User Journey

Stage 1 - Discovery through PPC

Imagine a user, let's call her Sarah, who's in search of a stylish backpack for her upcoming travels. She types" best travel backpacks" into a search engine, and your PPC ad catches her eye. The ad's captivating imagery and compelling offer pique her interest, prompting her to click through to your website.

Stage 2 - Exploration with SEO

Sarah lands on a dedicated product page showcasing a range of travel back-packs. This page, skillfully optimized for SEO, not only showcases the backpacks' features and benefits but also offers in-depth guides on choosing the perfect travel companion. Sarah is intrigued by your expert advice and spends time exploring your website.

Stage 3 - Engagement through social media

As Sarah continues her research, she remembers the social media platforms she frequents. Curious, she checks her Instagram feed and finds your brand's profile. The captivating visuals and user-generated content featuring your backpacks resonate with her desire for authenticity. She follows your account, instantly connecting with your brand's personality.

Stage 4 - Decision and Conversion with PPC and SEO

After contemplating her options, Sarah is ready to decide. She returns to the search engine and types the specific model she's interested in. Thanks to your SEO efforts, your product page ranks high. Simultaneously, she's retargeted by your PPC ad, reminding her of the special discount you're offering. Convinced by the wealth of information and the incentive, she clicks through and completes her purchase.

Stage 5 - Post-Purchase Nurturing through social media and SEO

The relationship doesn't end with the sale. Through social media, Sarah joins a community of like-minded travelers who share their experiences with your backpacks. Your brand's consistent presence on her social feed and her regular visits to your website, which is enriched with valuable post purchase guides, solidify her trust in your brand.

Stage 6 - Advocacy and Loyalty

Delighted with her purchase and impressed by the seamless user journey, Sarah becomes a vocal advocate for your brand. She leaves positive reviews, engages with your social media content, and recommends your backpacks to her friends. Her loyalty transforms her from a customer into an ambassador, spreading positive word-of-mouth across the digital landscape.

Conclusion: A synchronized Symphony of Success

The synergy of PPC, SEO, and social media marketing isn't just about simultaneous implementation; it's about orchestrating a journey that guides users from discovery to loyalty. By crafting a perfect user journey that seamlessly integrates these three pillars, you're able to provide value at every touchpoint, cater to diverse user behaviors, and create a dynamic experience that leaves a lasting impression. This holistic approach transforms mere consumers into brand advocates, turning your marketing efforts into a symphony of success that resonates long after the final note has been played.

Chapter 2

The Pillars of Digital Marketing

2.1 PPC (Pay-Per-Click) Advertising - Navigating Google Ads and Microsoft Advertising

Pay-Per-Click (PPC) advertising stands as a dynamic powerhouse that delivers targeted visibility and tangible results. As a digital marketing manager, you understand that harnessing the potential of platforms like Google Ads and Microsoft Advertising requires not just technical know-how, but a strategic mindset that navigates challenges and leverages benefits for optimal campaign success.

Understanding Google Ads and Microsoft Advertising

Google Ads

The juggernaut of PPC advertising, Google Ads places your brand at the forefront of user searches, whether they're hunting for information, products, or services. With a variety of ad formats and targeting options, Google Ads offers unparalleled access to a vast audience.

Microsoft Advertising

Don't overlook the potential of Microsoft Advertising. Operating on Bing, Yahoo, and other Microsoft platforms, this alternative avenue can often be less competitive while still delivering substantial reach.

Benefits of PPC Advertising

Precise Targeting

PPC campaigns allow you to define your audience with meticulous precision, from demographics and location to interests and behaviors. This ensures that your ad reaches those most likely to engage with your content.

Immediate Visibility

Unlike SEO, which requires time to climb rankings, PPC provides instant visibility. Your ad is displayed right at the top, grabbing attention right where users are actively searching.

Measurable Results

The data-rich environment of PPC advertising empowers you to measure your campaign's success with tangible metrics like clicks, conversions, and ROI. This data guides your strategy refinement.

Flexibility

PPC campaigns offer flexibility in terms of budget, timing, and targeting. This adaptability means you can tailor your campaigns to align with your goals and audience behavior.

Remarketing

Remarketing enables you to re-engage users who have interacted with your brand before. This boosts brand recall and encourages conversion.

Challenges of PPC Advertising

Cost

Depending on your industry and keywords, PPC advertising can be costly, especially if you're bidding on competitive terms. Proper budget management is crucial.

Competition

The digital landscape is brimming with advertisers vying for the same audience. This saturation can drive up costs and make it challenging to stand out.

Keyword Research Complexity

The right keywords are the backbone of a successful PPC campaign. Researching and selecting the most effective keywords require meticulous analysis and ongoing adjustment.

Ad Fatigue

Users can grow weary of seeing the same ads repeatedly, leading to decreased engagement. Regularly refreshing your ad creatives is essential.

Performance Max Campaign and the AI Revolution

A Performance Max campaign is a cutting-edge solution offered by Google Ads. It's designed to maximize your reach across multiple Google platforms using a single campaign. Utilizing a variety of ad formats, it optimizes placements and targeting to reach users at every touchpoint, from YouTube and Search to Display and Discover.

AI and Machine Learning: Pioneering the Future of PPC

The future of PPC advertising lies in the embrace of AI and machine learning. Google Ads and Microsoft Advertising are increasingly powered by sophisticated algorithms that optimize bids, ad placements, and targeting. These technologies analyze vast amounts of data in real time, enabling campaigns to adapt and evolve with remarkable precision. AI-driven automation saves time, improves efficiency, and enhances performance. Smart bidding strategies, like Target CPA, conversion value and maximize conversions, optimize campaigns for specific goals, enabling you to focus on strategic decisions rather than mundane tasks.

Conclusion: Navigating the PPC Landscape with Foresight

Mastering PPC advertising involves not just tactical maneuvers but strategic foresight. Google Ads and Microsoft Advertising offer incredible potential, but success requires understanding their benefits and navigating their challenges. As you embark on the journey of crafting compelling ad creatives, strategic targeting, and leveraging AI-driven automation, you position your brand to harness the true power of PPC. This journey is a dynamic one, as the landscape evolves, and AI becomes an even more integral part of the equation. With the right approach, PPC advertising becomes a vessel that propels your brand towards unprecedented visibility and conversion rates in the digital realm.

2.2 Unleashing the Power of PPC Advertising includes Paid Social

In the bustling world of digital marketing, where attention spans are fleeting and competition is fierce, the allure of instant visibility and pinpoint targeting precision has transformed Pay-Per-Click (PPC) advertising into a dynamic force that can make or break a brand's online presence. As a digital marketing manager, you're keenly aware that the ability to command immediate attention and connect with the right audience is where the true magic of PPC lies.

Instant Visibility: Lighting Up the Digital Sky

Imagine you're on a busy street, and there's a giant billboard right at eye level showcasing your brand's message. This is the essence of instant visibility in the digital realm. With PPC advertising, your brand's message, whether it's a compelling ad copy, a stunning visual, or a tempting offer, is placed right at the top of search results, social media feeds, or relevant websites.

Search Engine Dominance

When users search for keywords related to your business, your ad appears prominently at the top of the search results. This prime real estate immediately captures their attention, increasing the likelihood of engagement.

Social Media Impact

On social platforms, your ad can appear seamlessly in users' feeds, ensuring it's seen as they scroll through their friends' updates and posts. This immediate presence in their online social experience is a powerful way to create brand recognition.

Display Network Influence

Through display ads, your brand can pop up on websites relevant to your industry. Users who are exploring articles or content related to your offerings are met with your ad, enhancing your reach in an environment they're already interested in.

Targeting Precision: The Bullseye Approach

The key to efficient and impactful marketing lies in reaching the right audience. Enter targeting precision, a feature of PPC advertising that enables you to define your audience with incredible accuracy.

Demographics

You can narrow down your audience based on age, gender, marital status, and more. If you're promoting a skincare brand, for instance, you can target females aged 25-40 with specific skincare concerns.

Geographical Targeting

Geo-targeting lets you focus on users within a particular region. Whether you're a local business or an e-commerce giant, this precision ensures your ads reach users where your offerings are most relevant.

Interest-Based Targeting

By analyzing user behavior and interests, you can tailor your ads to individuals who have shown interest in topics closely related to your business. If you sell fitness gear, you can target users who frequent health and wellness websites.

Keyword Relevance

In search engine PPC, targeting keywords is the essence. By bidding on specific keywords, you ensure your ads appear when users are actively seeking products or information related to those keywords.

The Power Couple: Instant Visibility and Targeting Precision

The synergy of instant visibility and targeting precision is where the true magic of PPC advertising comes alive. Imagine your skincare brand's ad appearing instantly when a user searches for" best anti-aging creams," and this user falls within your demographic and geographical targeting. The impact is twofold – immediate attention and relevance.

Conclusion: A Dual-Edged Sword of Success

In the fast-paced digital world, capturing attention and relevance are paramount, and PPC advertising equips you with the dual-edged sword of instant visibility and targeting precision. By strategically placing your brand's message in the spotlight and ensuring it resonates with those most likely to engage, you're able to create a powerful connection that drives not just clicks, but meaningful interactions. As you continue to master the art of instant visibility and targeting precision, your campaigns transcend mere advertisements and become the catalysts for lasting brand impact in the minds and hearts of your audience.

2.3   Adapting to New Search Engine Updates

Navigating Ad Blockers and Mitigating Risks in PPC Advertising

One of the most significant challenges that has emerged in recent times is the rise of ad blockers. As a digital marketing manager, you understand that adapting to new search engine updates, particularly in the face of ad blockers, is not just essential, but a testament to your ability to navigate risks and seize opportunities. The Ad blockers are browser extensions or software that users install to prevent ads from displaying on websites. This stems from users' desire for a seamless and uninterrupted online experience. However, this practice poses a unique challenge to PPC advertising, as it restricts the very channel that provides instant visibility.

The Risks: Navigating choppy Waters

Visibility and Reach Reduction

Ad blockers severely limit the reach of your PPC campaigns. Your carefully crafted ads may not even reach a substantial portion of your intended audience, hindering your visibility and potential conversions.

Budget Drain

Your budget allocation for PPC advertising could be less effective due to the restricted reach caused by ad blockers. You might be investing resources in ads that aren't even being displayed to a significant segment of your audience.

Decline in Click-Through Rates (CTR)

Users who do not see ads may not click on them, leading to a decline in your campaign's click-through rates. This affects the overall effectiveness of your campaigns and potentially impacts your Quality Score.

Mitigating Risks and Seizing Opportunities

Creating Non-Intrusive Ads

As a response to ad blockers, consider crafting ads that align with users' preferences for non-intrusive content. Focus on creating valuable and engaging content that users might be less inclined to block.

Native Advertising

Native ads blend seamlessly with the surrounding content, making them less likely to be flagged by ad blockers. This approach enhances user experience while maintaining your brand's visibility.

Diversified Content

Expand your digital presence beyond traditional ads. Invest in content marketing, influencer collaborations, and social media engagement. By diversifying your approach, you reduce reliance on traditional ads.

Quality over Quantity

Shift your focus from bombarding users with ads to delivering fewer, high-quality ads. This approach can help improve engagement and prevent user alienation.

Leveraging First-Party Data

Utilize your own customer data to target users who have previously engaged positively with your brand. These users are more likely to have whitelisted your content.

Transparency and Value Exchange

Communicate the value users receive from viewing your ads. If users perceive a fair value exchange, they might be less inclined to block your content.

Conclusion: Navigating Ad Blockers with Innovation and Adaptability

In the face of ad blockers and new search engine updates, the key lies in innovation and adaptability. While these challenges might reshape the landscape of PPC advertising, they also present an opportunity for creativity. By focusing on user experience, value exchange, and diversification, you not only navigate the risks but also carve out a unique path that positions your brand as a champion of a more user centric digital ecosystem. In this ever-evolving journey, the ability to adapt is not just a necessity; it's the hallmark of a visionary digital marketing manager who thrives in the face of change.

2.4 The Rise of Search Generative Experience

Transforming PPC Strategies, Challenges, and Advantages

The emergence of the Search Generative Experience represents a significant shift that directly impacts the landscape of PPC advertising. As an adept digital marketing manager, understanding the implications, navigating the pain points, and harnessing the benefits of this evolution is essential to crafting successful PPC strategies in this new era.

Understanding Search Generative Experience

The Search Generative Experience is a paradigm shift in how users interact with search engines. It's a transition from users providing specific queries to search engines generating responses based on broader prompts. This shift is powered by advancements in Natural Language Processing (NLP) and machine learning, creating more conversational and intuitive interactions.

Challenges for PPC Marketers

Keyword Precision Challenges

With users providing broader prompts, keyword targeting becomes intricate. Traditional keyword strategies may need to evolve to capture the intent behind open-ended queries.

Ad Relevance and Matching

Generating ads that align with the context of dynamically generated search results becomes more challenging. Ensuring your ads resonate with these context-driven responses is essential.

Ad Copy and Creatives

Adapting ad copy to align with dynamic prompts demands a more flexible and real-time approach. Crafting compelling ad creatives that match the conversational context is a new challenge.

User Intent Deciphering

Understanding the underlying intent behind open-ended queries requires a deeper analysis of user behavior, preferences, and trends. This requires refined audience insights.

Benefits for PPC Marketers

Enhanced User Engagement

The Search Generative Experience fosters more natural and engaging interactions. This translates to more focused and relevant engagement with your ads.

Opportunity for Creativity

This shift encourages creativity in ad copy and strategy. Brands that can seamlessly integrate into dynamic search results have a higher chance of standing out.

Access to New Audiences

Users who engage with open-ended queries might fall outside traditional keyword targeting. The Search Generative Experience allows you to tap into new audience segments.

Data Insights Enrichment

By understanding the nuances of user-generated prompts, you gain deeper insights into user intent and preferences. This data enriches your overall marketing strategy.

First-Mover Advantage

As the Search Generative Experience is still evolving, being an early adopter positions you as a pioneer, giving you an edge over competitors.

Adapting PPC Strategies for the Search Generative Experience

Contextual Ad Copy

Develop ad copy that resonates with dynamic search responses. Focus on crafting versatile ad creatives that can adapt to various user-generated prompts.

Intent-Driven Keywords

Instead of just keywords, focus on user intent. Think about the questions users might ask to generate the prompts and tailor your keyword strategy accordingly.

Data Utilization

Leverage user data to understand conversational patterns and preferences. This informs your ad targeting and creative optimization.

AI-Powered Optimization

Embrace AI and machine learning tools to analyze the evolving search landscape and adjust your campaigns in real time.

Conclusion: Embracing the Evolution with Foresight

The Rise of Search Generative Experience marks a shift that challenges traditional PPC strategies while offering unique avenues for engagement and growth. As a digital marketing manager, embracing this evolution requires a blend of adaptability and innovation. By recognizing the challenges and capitalizing on the benefits, you position your brand to thrive in this dynamic landscape, crafting PPC strategies that seamlessly integrate with users' natural interactions and generate meaningful results.

2.5 SEO (Search Engine Optimization)

Unveiling SEO's Potential in a World of Generative Search: Navigating the Landscape of Evolving User Interactions

In the ever-evolving realm of digital marketing, the emergence of generative search marks a transformative shift in how users interact with search engines. As a seasoned digital marketing manager, understanding the unfolding landscape and harnessing the potential of SEO within this paradigm is crucial for positioning your brand at the forefront of this dynamic evolution.

The Dynamics of Generative Search

Generative search introduces a new dimension to user interactions, where search engines utilize advanced language models and artificial intelligence to generate responses based on open-ended prompts. This transition from traditional keyword-based search to more conversational and context-driven interactions reshape the SEO landscape.

Unveiling SEO's Potential

Semantic Search Optimization

Generative search thrives on understanding the context of user queries. Semantic search optimization becomes paramount. Focus shifts from individual keywords to concepts and intent. By crafting content that addresses broader themes and intent, you align with the generative nature of search, increasing the likelihood of being featured in dynamically generated responses.

User-Centric Content Creation

Generative search emphasizes understanding user intent and providing valuable content. Create content that answers common questions and addresses users' pain points. Long-form content that comprehensively covers a topic is more likely to match the depth of user-generated prompts.

Natural Language and Conversational SEO

As users interact with search engines conversationally, your content should mirror this natural language. Incorporate long tail and conversational keywords. Focus on creating content that reads organically while still addressing key search queries.

Structured Data and Snippets

Structured data markup becomes an asset in the generative search era. It provides context to search engines about your content's key elements. Featured snippets, which are often generated in response to user queries, can enhance your visibility and authority.

Adaptive Content Optimization

Generative search leads to dynamic shifts in search results. Continuously monitor search trends and updates. Adapt your content optimization strategies to align with evolving generative search patterns.

Voice Search Integration

Voice search and generative search share common ground in their emphasis on natural language. Optimize for voice search by focusing on question-based content and addressing user queries directly.

Challenges and Opportunities

Increased Competition for Featured Responses

As search engines generate responses, the competition to be featured in those responses intensifies. Strategic content creation and optimization become essential to secure a spot.

Personalization and User Intent

Understanding user intent and delivering personalized content gains prominence. Tailor your content to cater to specific queries and preferences.

Navigating Evolving Algorithms

Generative search relies heavily on AI and machine learning. Stay updated on algorithm changes and adjustments. AI-powered tools can aid in identifying patterns and optimizing content accordingly.

Local Search Optimization

With location playing a pivotal role in generative search, local businesses should emphasize local SEO strategies. Optimize for" near me" queries and ensure your business information is accurate.

The Rise of Visual Search

As visual search gains traction, optimizing images and visual content becomes crucial. Alt text, image descriptions, and schema markup enhance your visibility in generative visual search results.

Conclusion: Pioneering SEO in the Generative Search Era

In the world of generative search, SEO transcends its traditional boundaries, becoming a dynamic fusion of semantic understanding, conversational optimization, and context-driven content creation. By embracing these shifts and adapting your strategies to align with the new search landscape, you position your brand as a pioneer in catering to users' evolving interactions. As a digital marketing manager, you hold the key to unveiling SEO's potential and guiding your brand towards sustained visibility and authority in this exciting era of generative search.

2.6   Organic Reach and Long-Term Credibility

In the labyrinthine landscape of digital marketing, the ascent of generative search heralds a new era that magnifies the significance of organic reach and long-term credibility. As an accomplished digital marketing manager, delving even deeper into the profound implications of these concepts is pivotal, guiding you to chart a course that not only aligns with generative search dynamics but also establishes your brand's lasting foothold in the digital realm.

The Intricacies of Organic Reach

Organic reach epitomizes the genuine connection your content forges with users, free from the confines of paid promotion. Generative search's emphasis on context and user intent amplifies the essence of organic reach, enabling your content to organically resonate with users seeking information, solutions, and experiences.

Navigating the Seas of Long-Term Credibility

Long-term credibility stands as the bedrock of sustainable digital success. In the realm of generative search, credibility takes on new dimensions as search engines prioritize authoritative and reliable sources in dynamically generated responses.

The Power of Organic Reach in Generative Search

User-Centric Intent Alignment

Organic reach's true potency lies in its ability to seamlessly align with user intent. By crafting content that genuinely addresses users' needs and queries, you not only enhance your visibility in generative responses but also establish a profound connection with your audience.

Contextual Resonance

Generative search thrives on context. Organic reach ensures your content speaks the language of the user's context, enhancing the chances of being featured in dynamically generated responses.

Depth and Comprehensive Information

Generative search often seeks comprehensive answers. Organic reach empowers you to delve into a topic, providing in-depth insights that align with the information-hungry nature of generative queries.

Forging Long-Term Credibility in the Generative Era

Content Authority and Expertise

Long-term credibility hinges on positioning your brand as an authority in your niche. Create content that showcases your expertise, consistently delivering value that resonates with both users and search engines.

Earning Quality Backlinks

Backlinks remain a cornerstone of credibility. Prioritize earning high-quality, relevant backlinks from authoritative sources to reinforce your standing in the digital ecosystem.

User Experience and Engagement

Credibility extends to user experience. Engage users with intuitive navigation, fast-loading pages, and seamless mobile optimization to signify your brand's commitment to user satisfaction.

Transparency and Authenticity

In the era of generative search, authenticity reigns supreme. Transparent practices, genuine reviews, and open communication bolster your credibility.

Consistency in Content

Long-term credibility is cultivated through consistent content creation. Regularly publishing valuable content underscores your commitment to staying relevant and informative.

Balancing Organic Reach and Long-Term Credibility

The synergy between organic reach and long-term credibility forms the cornerstone of your SEO strategy in the generative search era.

Strategic Content Amplification

Amplify your content through targeted promotion and distribution while ensuring its core message retains.

Thought Leadership Content

Embrace thought leadership content that establishes your brand as a reliable source of industry insights and expertise, contributing to long-term credibility.

Quality Over Quantity

Prioritize quality content over volume. A select number of authoritative pieces align with long-term credibility while also catering to generative search's demand for depth.

Conclusion: Navigating the Nexus of Reach and Credibility

The journey through generative search's impact on SEO unveils a path where organic reach and long-term credibility intertwine. By orchestrating a harmonious balance between content that organically resonates with users' intent and content that asserts your brand's authority, you not only excel in this new era but also lay the foundation for a lasting digital legacy. Your mastery lies in forging this delicate nexus, elevating your brand's position in the generative search landscape, and ensuring your voice resounds with authenticity and impact.

2.7 Navigating the Depths of Search Engine Algorithm Shifts: Adapting SEO Strategies in the Age of Generative Search

In the intricate labyrinth of digital marketing, the tides of search engine algorithms ebb and flow, shaping the landscape in which brands vie for visibility and prominence. As a seasoned digital marketing manager, diving even deeper into the intricate realm of search engine algorithm shifts is imperative, enabling you to orchestrate strategies that navigate the currents of change and anchor your brand's success amidst the dynamic waves of generative search.

The Unpredictable Symphony of Algorithm Shifts

Search engine algorithms, the algorithms that determine how search results are displayed, are like symphonies that evolve over time. In the era of generative search, where context and user intent reign supreme, algorithm shifts are more intricate and dynamic than ever before.

Adapting to Algorithmic Nuances

Semantic Understanding and Intent Matching

Generative search values semantic understanding and intent matching. Tailor your content to not only include relevant keywords but also align with the context and intent behind user queries.

Contextual Optimization

Algorithms are now more adept at understanding context. Optimize your content for a broader range of keywords and phrases related to your topic to capture the breadth of user intent.

User-Centric Experience

Algorithms increasingly reward user-centric experiences. Focus on fast loading pages, mobile-friendliness, and intuitive navigation to ensure positive user experiences.

Strategies to Navigate Algorithm Shifts

Continuous Monitoring and Adaptation

Regularly monitor algorithm updates and their impacts on your rankings. Be ready to adapt your strategies to align with new ranking factors and criteria.

Data-Driven Insights

Leverage data analytics to track the performance of your content across various algorithm shifts. Identify patterns and trends to refine your approach.

Holistic Content Strategy

Develop a comprehensive content strategy that encompasses a mix of for- mats—long-form articles, videos, infographics—to cater to diverse user preferences.

Machine Learning and AI Tools

Utilize AI-powered tools to analyze shifts in search behavior and predict potential algorithm changes. Adjust your strategies proactively based on these insights.

Mitigating Algorithmic Risks

Diversification of Traffic Sources

Relying solely on organic search can be risky. Diversify your traffic sources through social media, email marketing, and other channels to mitigate potential drops in rankings due to algorithm shifts.

Focus on Long-Term Value

Avoid chasing short-term ranking gains by employing black-hat tactics. Focus on building long-term value through high-quality, authoritative content.

Capitalizing on Algorithmic Opportunities

Voice Search Optimization

Algorithm shifts are often influenced by the rise of voice search. Optimize for voice queries by tailoring your content to conversational language patterns.

Rich Snippets and Structured Data

Algorithmic shifts increasingly favor content that appears as rich snippets. Incorporate structured data markup to enhance your content's chances of being featured.

Conclusion: Sailing Through Algorithmic Seas with Expertise

In the intricate dance between search engine algorithms and SEO strategies, success lies in your ability to navigate the shifting tides with expertise and agility. By understanding the nuances of algorithm shifts, anticipating potential changes, and crafting strategies that prioritize user intent, context, and value, you craft a course that guides your brand to prominence in the generative search landscape. Your mastery lies in this navigation, ensuring your brand's resonance persists amidst the ever-changing currents of the algorithmic ocean.

2.8   Post-Pandemic Search Behavior

Unveiling the Evolution of Post-Pandemic Search Behavior: Crafting SEO Strategies for a Transformed Digital Landscape

In the wake of the global pandemic, the digital landscape has undergone a seismic shift, with search behavior evolving in profound ways. As an astute digital marketing manager, diving even deeper into the intricate evolution of post-pandemic search behavior unveils critical insights that empower you to recalibrate SEO strategies and navigate this transformed terrain with foresight and precision.

A New Dawn of Search Behavior

The pandemic catalyzed a rapid digital transformation, redefining how individuals interact with the online world. Remote work, e-commerce surges, and a heightened reliance on digital solutions have all contributed to reshaping the way users search, seek information, and engage with brands.

Understanding the Evolution

Local Intent and E-commerce Surge

Local searches surged as users sought nearby products and services due to mobility restrictions. The rise of e-commerce transformed how users' shop, emphasizing the need for local optimization and seamless online purchasing experiences.

Virtual Experiences and Online Learning

Virtual events, webinars, and online learning became the norm. Users now seek engaging virtual experiences, prompting a shift in content strategies to accommodate this demand.

Health and Wellness Focus

Health-related searches soared as users sought information on immunity, wellness, and safety measures. Brands catering to health and wellness found themselves in high demand.

Strategies for the Transformed Landscape

Localized Optimization

Prioritize local SEO to capture users seeking nearby solutions. Optimize Google My Business profiles, local directories, and tailor content to address local intent.

E-Commerce Enhancement

Bolster your e-commerce strategies. Optimize product pages, provide detailed descriptions, leverage customer reviews, and ensure seamless checkout experiences.

Virtual Engagement

Craft content that fosters virtual engagement, such as webinars, virtual tours, and live streams. Tailor your content to provide immersive experiences that resonate with remote audiences.

Health and Well-being Content

Embrace health and wellness content. Provide credible information, offer expert insights, and align your brand with the growing interest in holistic well-being.

Mitigating Search Behavior Challenges

Adaptability

Rapid shifts in search behavior require nimbleness. Continuously monitor trends, analyze user behavior, and adapt your strategies accordingly.

Content Relevance

Align content with the evolving interests and concerns of users. Anticipate their questions, offer solutions, and stay ahead of the curve.

Harnessing Search Behavior Opportunities

Personalization

Leverage user data to personalize content and experiences. Tailor recommendations, offers, and suggestions based on individual preferences.

Voice Search Optimization

As voice search gains prominence, optimize your content for natural language queries, aiming to capture the conversational nature of voice interactions.

Conclusion: Sterring SEO Strategies with Insight

The post-pandemic evolution of search behavior is a testament to the digital landscape's resilience and adaptability. By delving into the intricacies of this transformation, you unearth the keys to recalibrating SEO strategies that resonate with the new demands and expectations of users. Your expertise lies in steering your brand through this transformed landscape, aligning your strategies with the evolving needs of users, and solidifying your brand's presence in the hearts and minds of a digitally transformed audience.

2.9   Social Media Marketing

Harnessing Social Media's Impact

In the modern digital ecosystem, the pervasive influence of social media has become a cornerstone of brand visibility, engagement, and connection. As a seasoned digital marketing manager, delving into the depths of harnessing social media's impact provides invaluable insights that can elevate your strategies to new heights. This exploration not only uncovers the nuances of effective social media utilization but also underscores its pivotal role in shaping brand narratives, fostering communities, and driving conversions.

Understanding Social Media's Role

Social media has evolved beyond a mere communication tool; it's now a powerful vehicle for brand storytelling, customer engagement, and community building. Its real-time nature allows brands to foster authentic relationships, directly connect with audiences, and showcase their values in action.

The Power of Storytelling and Engagement

Authentic Narratives

Successful brands weave authentic narratives that resonate with their core values. TOMS, a shoe company, uses social media to share their One for One program, where every purchase supports a person in need.

Influencer Partnerships

Collaborating with influencers extends your reach to their engaged followers. Gymshark, a fitness apparel brand, strategically partners with fitness influencers to amplify their brand messaging.

User-Generated Content (UGC)

Encouraging users to create content around your brand fosters a sense of community. Starbucks' White Cup Contest prompted customers to decorate their cups, generating thousands of UGC posts.

Community Building and Customer Support

Engagement Groups

Nurturing engagement groups or forums for enthusiasts enables them to connect and share their experiences. Harley-Davidson's H.O.G. (Harley Owners Group) community brings together passionate riders.

Real-Time Customer Support

Brands like Zappos excel in using social media for swift customer support, addressing inquiries promptly and enhancing customer satisfaction.

Driving Conversions and Sales

Shoppable Posts

Platforms like Instagram enable direct product tagging, leading users from discovery to purchase seamlessly. Fashion brand ASOS utilizes shoppable posts to turn inspiration into action.

Limited-Time Offers

Posting time-sensitive offers exclusively on social media compels users to take immediate action. Domino's Pizza leverages this strategy with flash discounts.

Leveraging Data for Precision

Analytics Insights

Platforms provide detailed analytics on audience behavior. Netflix, for instance, utilizes data to understand viewer preferences and tailors content recommendations.

Targeted Advertising

Social media's targeting options enable precision in reaching specific demographics. Airbnb uses demographic and interest-based targeting to showcase relevant property listings.

Navigating Challenges and Adapting

Algorithm Changes

Platforms' algorithms evolve, impacting reach. Brands must adapt by diversifying content types and engaging with trending topics.

Negative Feedback

Negative comments and backlash can occur. Swift, empathetic responses demonstrate brand accountability. Wendy's humorous responses to customer comments showcase effective management.

Seizing Opportunities and Staying Innovative

Video Dominance

Video content reigns supreme. YouTube shorts & Tik Tok rise exemplifies the potential of short-form videos in capturing attention and sparking trends.

Social Commerce

E-commerce integration within platforms transforms social media into a shopping hub. Facebook Marketplace is an example of a platform bridging social interactions and transactions.

Conclusion: Unleashing the Potential of Social Media Mastery

Delving deep into the world of harnessing social media's impact uncovers a realm where engagement, community, storytelling, and conversion converge. By employing storytelling prowess, fostering authentic connections, embracing data-driven insights, and staying adaptive in the face of challenges, you wield social media as a transformative force that shapes brand perceptions, fuels engagement, and drives tangible results. Your journey involves unraveling this multifaceted impact and steering your brand's narrative towards resonance, influence, and enduring success.

2.10 Building Brand Awareness and Loyalty

Illuminating the Path to Building Lasting Brand Awareness and Loyalty: A Comprehensive Dive into Strategies for Meaningful Impact

In the intricate realm of digital marketing, the pursuit of brand awareness and loyalty transcends conventional metrics, encompassing the art of fostering genuine connections, resonating with audiences, and nurturing unwavering brand allegiance. As an adept digital marketing manager, embarking on an immersive exploration of building brand awareness and loyalty unveils strategies that not only amplify your brand's visibility but also cultivate emotional bonds, inspire advocacy, and cultivate a legacy of trust and loyalty.

Understanding the Essence of Brand Awareness

Consistent Visual Identity

Develop a consistent visual identity across platforms. Apple's iconic logo and minimalist design elements instantly resonate with its brand.

Authentic Storytelling

Craft a compelling brand story that encapsulates your journey, values, and mission. Patagonia's commitment to environmental sustainability is a prime example.

Crafting Strategies for Sustained Loyalty

Personalized Experiences

Tailor experiences based on user preferences. Amazon's product recommendations based on browsing history exemplify personalized loyalty-building tactics.

Customer-Centric Approach

Focus on customer needs and delight. Zappos' renowned customer service not only solves issues but fosters loyalty through positive interactions.

Empowering Emotional Connections

Emotional Branding

Foster emotional connections by evoking feelings. Dove's" Real Beauty" campaign challenges beauty standards, resonating with diverse audiences.

Cause Marketing

Align your brand with meaningful causes. Starbucks' commitment to ethically sourced coffee connects with socially conscious consumers.

Effective Engagement Strategies

Storytelling through Content

Share relatable stories through blogs, videos, and social media. Coca-Cola's" Share a Coke" campaign sparks conversations through personalized labels.

Interactive Campaigns

Encourage user participation. Lay's" Do Us a Flavor" campaign invites consumers to create and vote on new chip flavors.

Fostering Advocacy and User-Generated Content (UGC)

Loyalty Programs

Reward loyal customers with exclusive perks. Starbucks' rewards program offers free drinks and discounts to incentivize repeat business.

UGC Contests

Engage users by inviting them to create content. GoPro's UGC contests encourage users to share their thrilling adventures captured on their cameras.

Precision in Loyalty Measurement

Net Promoter Score (NPS)

Measure loyalty with NPS surveys, gauging how likely customers are to recommend your brand to others.

Customer Lifetime Value (CLV)

Calculate the long-term value of loyal customers. Apple's ecosystem thrives on repeat purchases, showcasing the impact of brand loyalty.

Staying Adaptive and Evolving

Feedback Integration

Listen to customer feedback and evolve accordingly. Netflix constantly refines its content based on user viewing preferences.

Competitor Analysis

Analyze competitors to identify gaps in the market. Airbnb revolutionized the travel industry by offering unique homestay experiences.

Conclusion: Forging a Legacy of Brand Excellence

Deepening your exploration into the intricacies of building brand awareness and loyalty unveils a realm where authenticity, emotional resonance, and customer-centricity intersect. By employing strategies that transcend transactional interactions, you orchestrate an enduring narrative that resonates with audiences, fosters advocacy, and weaves lasting loyalty. Your journey is one of nurturing connections that transcend screens, forging a legacy of brand excellence that stands as a beacon of trust, loyalty, and profound impact.

2.11 Leveraging Gen Z's Values and Search Behavior

Decoding the Values and Behavior of Generation Z: A Profound Exploration into Connecting with the Heart of the Future

In the vast landscape of digital marketing, comprehending the values and behavior of Generation Z (Gen Z) is not merely a strategic choice but a profound necessity. As a discerning digital marketing manager, delving into the depths of Gen Z's mindset unveils a tapestry of values, preferences, and behaviors that shape their interactions with brands. This journey transcends demographics, reaching the very essence of this generation, and equips you with the insight to create authentic connections that resonate deeply and authentically.

Understanding the Values that Define Gen Z

Authenticity Gen Z craves authenticity in brands. They respond to genuine stories and transparent practices. Brands like Glossier exemplify this with minimal retouching of models in their beauty campaigns.

Social Impact

Environmental and social causes matter deeply to Gen Z. They align with brands that actively contribute to positive change. TOMS'" One for One" model resonates by donating shoes to those in need.

Behavioral Patterns that Shape Gen Z Engagement

Digital Natives

Gen Z is the first generation to grow up in a fully digital world. Their familiarity with technology and platforms makes them adept at discerning authentic content from mere marketing ploys.

Short Attention Spans

Gen Z's attention span is fleeting, demanding concise and engaging content. TikTok's success lies in its bite-sized, entertaining videos that cater to this preference.

Connecting through Gen Z's Lens

Visual Content

Utilize visually captivating content. Gen Z responds to visually appealing formats like videos, images, and infographics. Gymshark employs visually striking imagery to engage fitness enthusiasts.

User-Generated Content (UGC)

Encourage UGC to involve Gen Z in brand narratives. Dunkin' Donuts' #DunkinReplay campaign invited users to create their own dance, fostering engagement.

Embracing Diversity and Inclusivity

Cultural Sensitivity

Gen Z values diversity and inclusivity. Brands like Fenty Beauty excel by offering inclusive shade ranges that cater to people of all skin tones.

Representation

Showcasing a diverse range of models and individuals in campaigns fosters a sense of belonging. Adidas' collaborations with diverse influencers resonate with Gen Z's values.

Transparency and Ethical Practices

Supply Chain Transparency

Gen Z seeks ethical and sustainable practices. Brands like Everlane emphasize transparent supply chains, resonating with their desire for responsible consumption.

Corporate Responsibility

Brands that actively address social and environmental issues, like Patagonia's commitment to eco-friendly practices, align with Gen Z's values.

Adapting to Gen Z's Values

Purpose-Driven Messaging

Craft messages that align with causes Gen Z cares about. Nike's Colin Kaepernick campaign aligned with their stance on social justice.

Interactive Campaigns

Engage Gen Z with interactive campaigns. Doritos'" Another Level" campaign invited users to scan chips for unique augmented reality experiences.

Conclusion: Pioneering Authentic Connections with Gen Z

Delving deep into the values and behavior of Generation Z unearths a world where authenticity, social impact, and diversity are the guiding stars. By crafting strategies that resonate with their deeply held values, leveraging engaging content formats, and fostering genuine connections, you establish your brand as a trusted companion on their digital journey. Your role is one of empathy and insight, weaving narratives that mirror Gen Z's ethos, fostering connections that transcend transactions, and leaving an indelible imprint on a generation that stands as the harbinger of the future.

2.12 Embracing Authenticity and Engaging Content

A Profound Exploration with Exemplary Brands

In the ever-evolving realm of digital marketing, the pursuit of authenticity and engaging content has emerged as a linchpin for brand resonance and meaningful connections. As a discerning digital marketing manager, delving into the depths of authenticity and content creation unveils a landscape where genuine connections, transparency, and captivating narratives intersect. This journey is marked by a profound understanding of values, empathy, and the art of crafting content that not only captivates but also resonates with audiences on a profound level.

Transparent Brand Storytelling

Brands like Patagonia have masterfully embraced transparency, sharing their environmental initiatives and challenges, fostering a sense of authenticity that resonates with eco-conscious consumers.

Human-Centric Approach

Dove's" Real Beauty" campaign celebrated real women, shunning unrealistic beauty standards. This authentic representation resonated with a diverse audience, inspiring conversations about self-worth.

Creating Engaging Content that Resonates

Video Storytelling

Red Bull's adventure-filled videos transport viewers into exhilarating experiences, fostering emotional engagement, and aligning with their" gives you wings" ethos.

Interactive Experiences

IKEA's" Place" app lets users visualize furniture in their spaces using augmented reality, offering an interactive and practical engagement.

Exemplary Brands Embracing Authenticity

Ben & Jerry's

Known for its activism, Ben & Jerry's addresses social issues authentically. Their" Justice ReMix'd" flavor was launched to raise awareness about criminal justice reform.

Airbnb

Airbnb showcases real hosts and their unique spaces, epitomizing the platform's commitment to authentic travel experiences.

Humanizing Through Empathy

Connecting with Customers

Wendy's Twitter account employs witty, humorous responses to customer interactions, demonstrating a human side to the brand.

Storytelling Through User Journeys

Starbucks often shares stories of baristas' personal journeys, fostering empathy and connection with its employees and customers.

Transparency as the Foundation

Ethical Practices

Patagonia's" Don't Buy This Jacket" campaign challenged consumerism by urging customers to buy only what they need, aligning with their ethical stance.

Supply Chain Visibility

Everlane takes transparency to the next level, showcasing the factories where their products are made and disclosing the true cost of production.

Creating Engaging Narratives

Apple

Apple's" Shot on iPhone" campaign features user-generated photos, celebrating creativity and engaging the global community of iPhone users.

National Geographic

National Geographic's visual storytelling captures the beauty of the world and its diverse cultures, inspiring a sense of wonder and fostering engagement.

Conclusion: Forging a Legacy of Authenticity and Engagement Mastery

Delving deep into the realm of authenticity and engaging content creation uncovers a landscape where values, empathy, and genuine connections intertwine. By infusing your brand with authenticity, embracing transparency, and crafting narratives that resonate deeply, you establish your brand not just as a market player, but as a trusted companion on the consumer journey. Your role is that of a storyteller and empathetic guide, navigating the path where authenticity and engagement converge, leaving an indelible mark on the hearts and minds of audiences, just as exemplified by the trailblazing brands that have pioneered this journey.

Chapter 3

Cutting-Edge Innovations and Trends

3.1 Google Lens: Revolutionizing Visual Search

Unveiling the Power of Google Lens: Navigating Benefits and Challenges for Marketers with Exemplary Brand Implementations

In the dynamic landscape of digital marketing, Google Lens has emerged as a transformative tool that transcends traditional boundaries, bridging the gap between the physical and digital worlds. As a seasoned digital marketing manager, delving into the intricacies of Google Lens unveils a world of possibilities where visual search, augmented reality, and seamless interactions converge, redefining user engagement and brand experiences. This chapter offers a comprehensive exploration of the benefits, challenges, and exemplary brand implementations of Google Lens.

The Marvel of Google Lens

Google Lens, powered by advanced image recognition and machine learning, transforms smartphones into visual search engines. It enables users to explore the world through images, instantly identifying objects, text, landmarks, and even animals.

Benefits for Marketers

Enhanced User Engagement

Google Lens fosters interactive engagement, allowing users to discover more about products, services, and physical objects they encounter.

Seamless Discovery

Brands can leverage Google Lens to offer instant access to detailed information about products, simplifying the user journey from curiosity to purchase.

Augmented Reality Integration

Google Lens integrates augmented reality, allowing users to visualize products in real-world environments. IKEA's" Place" app, powered by Google Lens, enables users to virtually place furniture in their spaces.

Exemplary Brand Implementations

Pinterest

Pinterest integrates Google Lens to enable users to take a photo of an object and find visually similar pins, facilitating discovery and inspiration.

Sephora

Sephora utilizes Google Lens to enable users to scan products and instantly access makeup tutorials, product reviews, and purchase options.

Navigating Challenges for Marketers

Visual Optimization

Brands must optimize visuals for recognition, ensuring logos, products, and text are easily identifiable by Google Lens.

Privacy Concerns

Balancing convenience with privacy remains a challenge. Brands must ensure user data is handled responsibly and transparently.

Seizing Opportunities with Google Lens

Visual Search Optimization

Brands can optimize visuals on websites and social media for Google Lens, enhancing their discoverability and offering users rich contextual information.

Enhanced In-Store Experiences

Google Lens transforms physical spaces into interactive environments. Brands can create QR codes and visual triggers that offer additional information and exclusive offers when scanned with Google Lens.

Conclusion: Pioneering a Visual Frontier with Google Lens Mastery

Exploring the depths of Google Lens unveils a realm where visual search and augmented reality converge, shaping user interactions and brand experiences. By leveraging its capabilities, brands forge connections that transcend screens, creating seamless bridges between the digital and physical realms. Your role is to navigate this visual frontier, crafting strategies that harness the power of Google Lens to engage, inform, and captivate audiences in ways that redefine the essence of brand engagement. Just as Pinterest and Sephora have leveraged Google Lens to elevate their user experiences, you too can steer your brand toward new heights of visual engagement and innovation.

3.2 Incorporating Google Lens into Marketing Strategies

Mastering the Integration of Google Lens into Marketing Strategies: Elevating User Experiences with Exemplary Brand Success Stories

In the dynamic landscape of digital marketing, the integration of Google Lens into marketing strategies has emerged as a catalyst for reshaping user experiences and revolutionizing brand engagement. As a seasoned digital marketing manager, delving into the intricacies of incorporating Google Lens unveils a world where visual search, augmented reality, and seamless interactions converge, empowering brands to craft immersive narratives that resonate deeply. This chapter offers a profound exploration of strategies, benefits, challenges, and exemplary brand success stories that illuminate the path to Google Lens mastery.

Strategies for Seamless Integration

Visual Content Optimization

Brands must optimize visual assets across digital platforms to ensure easy recognition by Google Lens. This includes logos, product images, and packaging.

Interactive Print Materials

Integrate visual triggers, such as QR codes or markers, into print materials like brochures and catalogs. When scanned with Google Lens, these triggers provide additional information or exclusive offers.

Augmented Reality Experiences

Use Google Lens to enhance real-world experiences. Brands like IKEA create augmented reality apps that allow users to virtually place furniture in their spaces.

Benefits of Google Lens Integration

Enhanced Engagement

Google Lens offers interactive engagement, allowing users to explore products and gain detailed information instantly, fostering active engagement.

Seamless Discovery

Brands can provide users with immediate access to reviews, specifications, and purchase options by integrating Google Lens into their marketing materials.

Bringing Products to Life

Google Lens enables brands to create interactive experiences that bring products to life in consumers' physical environments, as seen in the success of the Sephora app.

Exemplary Brand Success Stories

Pinterest

By integrating Google Lens, Pinterest allows users to take photos of objects and discover visually similar pins, revolutionizing the way users discover inspiration.

Sephora

The Sephora app utilizes Google Lens to empower users to scan products and access makeup tutorials, reviews, and shopping options, elevating the beauty shopping experience.

Overcoming Challenges

Visual Optimization

Brands must ensure that visual assets are optimized for Google Lens recognition, ensuring accurate identification and information retrieval.

Privacy Considerations

Brands must address privacy concerns by transparently communicating data usage policies to users and obtaining necessary consents.

Creating Compelling Campaigns

Interactive Packaging

Brands can enhance product packaging with visual triggers that, when scanned, unveil interactive content, stories, or exclusive offers.

Educational Content

Educational campaigns can empower users with informative content. Brands can provide in-depth information about product ingredients, usage instructions, and more through Google Lens.

Conclusion: Forging a New Era of Visual Engagement with Google Lens Mastery

Unveiling the world of incorporating Google Lens into marketing strategies uncovers a realm where visual innovation, augmented reality, and user engagement intertwine. By infusing your strategies with Google Lens capabilities, you open doors to immersive experiences that captivate, educate, and resonate on a profound level. Your role is that of a visionary pioneer, crafting campaigns that not only leverage Google Lens to enhance brand engagement but also redefine the very essence of user experiences. Just as Pinterest and Sephora have harnessed Google Lens to elevate their brands, you too can chart a course toward a new era of visual engagement mastery.

3.3 Enhancing User Engagement through Visual Content

Unveiling the Nexus of Challenges and Benefits: Elevating User Engagement through Visual Content Mastery

In the dynamic realm of digital marketing, the pursuit of enhancing user engagement through visual content has emerged as a pivotal strategy that transcends conventional boundaries, captivating audiences and fostering deeper connections. As a digital marketing manager on a quest for profound insights, delving into the intricacies of this pursuit unveils a world where compelling visuals, storytelling prowess, and strategic integration converge. This chapter offers an immersive exploration, dissecting challenges, uncovering benefits, and providing a roadmap to mastering visual content for elevated user engagement.

Navigating the Terrain of Challenges

Content Overload

In an era of information saturation, capturing attention amidst the visual noise demands unparalleled creativity and originality.

Short Attention Spans

The fleeting attention spans of modern audiences necessitate visual content that communicates messages swiftly and effectively.

Platform-Specific Adaptation

Each digital platform requires tailored visual content, which can be time-consuming and resource intensive.

Beneath the Surface of Benefits

Emotional Resonance

Visual content has the power to evoke emotions and create lasting impressions, forming a deeper connection with the audience.

Information Absorption

Visuals facilitate rapid information absorption, making complex concepts digestible and enhancing user understanding.

Brand Identity Reinforcement

Consistent visual elements across content reinforce brand identity, enhancing recognition and fostering brand loyalty.

Addressing Challenges with Strategic Approaches

Creativity and Uniqueness

To stand out, infuse visual content with creativity and uniqueness that pique curiosity and inspire sharing.

Storytelling Excellence

Weave narratives within visual content to captivate audiences and provide context that resonates on a personal level.

Platform Optimization

Customize visual content for different platforms, adhering to each platform's format and preferences.

Leveraging Benefits for Engaging Content

Visual Storytelling

Craft narratives through visuals, as exemplified by Nike's emotionally charged advertisements that convey inspiring stories.

Infographics and Data Visualization

Simplify complex information through infographics and data visualization, as seen in The New York Times' interactive data-driven pieces.

User-Generated Content (UGC)

Encourage UGC to foster a sense of community and authenticity, as Starbucks does with its" White Cup Contest."

Exemplifying Success

Dove's" Real Beauty" Campaign

Dove's impactful campaign challenges beauty standards, resonating deeply with audiences and sparking conversations.

GoPro's User-Generated Content

GoPro's platform thrives on user-generated videos showcasing exhilarating adventures, building a passionate community.

Navigating Benefits with Wisdom

Audience-Centric Approach

Tailor visual content to match audience preferences, ensuring relevance and engagement.

Consistency and Frequency

Maintain a consistent posting schedule, providing audiences with regular doses of engaging visual content.

Conclusion: Pioneering Visual Content Excellence for Enduring Engagement

In the realm of enhancing user engagement through visual content, challenges and benefits intertwine to shape a dynamic landscape. Your role is that of a virtuoso conductor, orchestrating a symphony of creativity, strategy, and resonance. By addressing challenges with strategic finesse and embracing the benefits with unwavering wisdom, you harness the potential to cultivate user engagement that transcends screens, sparking conversations, building communities, and etching your brand into the hearts and minds of a visually driven audience.

3.4 Search Generative Experience and MUM

The Emergence of Search Generative Experience

Unveiling the search generative experience and its Impact on the digital marketing ecosystem. In the ever-evolving landscape of digital marketing, the emergence of the Search Generative Experience marks a paradigm shift that transcends traditional search paradigms, ushering in a new era of user-centric interaction and engagement. As a digital marketing visionary, plunging into the depths of this transformative phenomenon unravels a narrative where human-like interactions, convergence of channels, and user empowerment coalesce. This chapter embarks on a profound exploration, deciphering the essence of the Search Generative Experience, its implications on digital marketing, and the unprecedented potential that lies ahead.

The Essence of Search Generative Experience

The Search Generative Experience embodies a seismic shift from static keyword-based queries to conversational, intuitive interactions that mimic human thought processes. Powered by AI advancements, this new search era engages users in dynamic dialogues, yielding richer, contextual results that align with the intent behind their queries.

Unified Convergence of Digital Marketing Channels

Synergy Amplified

The Search Generative Experience blurs the boundaries between PPC, SEO, and social media. Integrating these channels harmoniously enhances brand visibility across various interaction touchpoints.

Holistic Optimization

Cross-channel optimization becomes paramount. Keywords, content, and ad targeting must align seamlessly to cater to the conversational nature of user queries.

Importance of Holistic Collaboration

Enhanced User Engagement

Collaborative efforts translate to consistent brand messaging, ensuring users receive coherent responses, regardless of the channel they engage with.

Deepened User Insights

Collaborative insights from PPC, SEO, and social media provide a comprehensive view of user behavior, empowering brands to tailor strategies.

User Benefits and Empowerment

Natural Interaction

Users engage in fluid, conversational dialogues, resulting in more relevant, context-aware search results.

Intuitive Discovery

The Search Generative Experience aids users in discovering answers, products, and services with an ease that mimics real-life conversations.

The Embryonic State and Future Promise

Early Dawn of Change

While the Search Generative Experience has already begun reshaping search, its full potential is yet to be realized, offering a glimpse into the transformative journey ahead.

Future Envisioned

The future holds promise of AI advancements that further comprehend nuances, delivering not just information, but personalized, emotionally resonant responses.

Exemplifying the Current Landscape

Google's BERT Update

Google's BERT update marked a stride towards understanding context in search queries, a precursor to the Search Generative Experience.

Chatbots and Virtual Assistants

Brands like Starbucks and Domino's employ chatbots that simulate humanlike interactions, offering a glimpse into the evolving landscape.

Navigating Forward: A Unified Digital Odyssey

As the digital marketing horizon evolves with the emergence of the Search Generative Experience, a cohesive narrative emerges. The intersection of PPC, SEO, and social media fosters an integrated approach, amplifying brand presence and nurturing authentic relationships. Amid this transformation, user empowerment reigns supreme, as interactions mirror real-life conversations, granting users the gift of intuitive discovery. While in its nascent stages, the Search Generative Experience holds the promise of an even more connected, insightful, and personalized future. As a digital marketing visionary, your role is that of a trailblazer, harnessing the power of unity across channels to steer your brand through this uncharted territory, crafting a symphony of interactions that resonate, empower, and illuminate the path ahead.

Mastering MUM: Multilingual and Multimodal Approach

In the ever-evolving landscape of digital marketing, the emergence of MUM (Multilingual and Multimodal Approach) stands as a pivotal juncture that redefines engagement, accessibility, and resonance on a global scale. As a digital marketing maestro poised on the cusp of innovation, embarking on an immersive exploration of MUM unravels a landscape where languages converge, visuals transcend, and user experiences become more profound. This chapter delves into the intricate tapestry of MUM, dissecting its facets, unraveling its significance, and providing a blueprint for mastery that amplifies your brand's digital impact.

Decoding MUM's Essence

MUM encapsulates the fusion of multilingualism and multimodal capabilities, enabling search engines to comprehend text, images, and context across languages seamlessly. This revolutionary stride empowers users to explore and connect in their preferred languages while embracing the language of visuals.

Elevating Engagement through Multimodal Power

Visual-Aided Search

MUM understands images and infuses them with contextual meaning, allowing users to find what they seek through visuals.

Text-to-Speech Dynamics

MUM's multimodal prowess empowers users to convert written text into spoken language, widening accessibility and engagement horizons.

Impact on Global Accessibility

Breaking Language Barriers

MUM transcends language borders, enabling users to explore content in their native languages, revolutionizing international user experiences.

Expanding Outreach

Brands can now tailor content to cater to diverse linguistic preferences, fostering inclusivity and resonating with a global audience.

Creating Multilingual and Multimodal Strategies

Multilingual SEO Optimization

Optimize content for multiple languages, focusing on keywords and context to enhance visibility across language-specific search queries.

Visual Storytelling

Leverage visuals to communicate universally, crafting narratives that transcend linguistic limitations and foster cross-cultural connections.

Exemplary Brand Success Stories

Google Translate

Google's multilingual prowess amplifies cross-border communication, allowing users to access content in their preferred languages.

Pinterest Visual Discovery

Pinterest's multimodal integration enables users to explore content through visuals, irrespective of language barriers.

Crafting a Future-Proof Strategy

Embrace Multilingual Content

Create content that resonates with diverse linguistic groups, aligning messages with cultural nuances.

Visual Metadata Optimization

Optimize visual content with metadata that transcends language, aiding MUM in providing context-rich results.

Personalized User Experiences

Localized Campaigns

Tailor campaigns to specific regions, embracing languages and visuals that resonate with local audiences.

Visual AI Integration

Harness visual AI tools to identify and tag objects within images, augmenting the multimodal experience.

Innovating on the Horizon

MUM's evolution is poised to reshape digital marketing dynamics further, introducing deeper context comprehension and improved user interactions. As MUM matures, brands can expect more precise and contextually aware results, offering users personalized, insightful, and linguistically rich experiences.

Conclusion: Forging a Global Legacy with Google MUM Mastery

Diving into the realm of MUM unveils a tapestry where languages blend and visuals converse, reshaping user experiences and brand narratives. Your role is to seize this moment of innovation, embracing MUM's capabilities to craft strategies that resonate across languages and cultures. By fostering inclusivity, breaking linguistic barriers, and harnessing the power of the visual, you cultivate a legacy that extends beyond borders, enriching user engagement and catalyzing exponential digital impact. Just as Google Translate and Pinterest have embraced MUM's potential, your journey toward MUM mastery propels your brand into a future where boundaries blur and connections thrive on a global scale.

3.5   Crafting Content for Next-Gen Search Experience

In the realm of digital marketing, the evolution of the next-gen search experience marks a watershed moment that demands an innovative approach to content creation. As a digital marketing luminary, embarking on a journey into crafting content for this new era unveils a realm where context, intent, and interactivity intertwine. This chapter delves deep into the challenges, possibilities, and exemplary brand success stories that illuminate the path to content mastery in the landscape of the next-gen search experience.

Challenges on the Content Horizon

Contextual Precision

Crafting content that aligns with nuanced user intent and context poses a challenge, demanding a shift from keyword-centric to intent-focused content creation.

Multimodal Fusion

Seamlessly integrating text, images, and potentially other forms of media to cater to the diverse ways users interact with content requires strategic planning.

Embracing the Potential of Next-Gen Search

Hyper-Relevance

Crafting content that precisely matches user intent results in hyper-relevant responses, fostering deeper engagement.

Visual Storytelling

Leveraging images, videos, and interactive media to tell compelling narratives adds layers of engagement to content.

Tailoring Content Strategies

Intent-Driven Optimization

Understand user intent across various stages of the buyer's journey and craft content that provides value at each touchpoint.

Visual Search Integration

Create visually appealing and contextually relevant images that enhance user engagement and interaction.

Exemplifying Content Brilliance

Sephora's Visual Search

Sephora's app leverages visual search, allowing users to explore products they discover in the real world by capturing images.

Pinterest's Dynamic Visual Discovery

Pinterest's algorithm adapts to user interactions, curating visually driven content that aligns with evolving preferences.

Enriching User Engagement

Interactive Content

Craft interactive quizzes, polls, and shoppable visuals that provide users with immersive, engaging experiences.

Voice-Optimized Content

Capitalize on voice search by crafting content that aligns with conversational queries, mirroring how users naturally speak.

Navigating the Frontier: Challenges as Opportunities

AI-Driven Insights

Utilize AI tools to understand user behavior, preferences, and search patterns, fueling data-backed content strategies.

Dynamic Adaptation

Continuously monitor search trends and adapt content strategies in Realtime to remain relevant and impactful.

Future-Proofing Content Creation

Contextual Personalization

Craft personalized content that resonates with user context, history, and preferences, creating more meaningful interactions.

Conversational Content Frameworks

Develop content that flows like a conversation, catering to voice search and natural language processing.

Conclusion: Pioneering Next-Gen Content Excellence

Embarking on the journey of crafting content for the next-gen search experience is a venture into uncharted territories where user intent, context, and interactivity reign supreme. Your role is that of a content architect, weaving narratives that transcend static text, resonating with users on a multi-dimensional level. By embracing challenges as opportunities, experimenting with interactive formats, and harnessing the power of visual storytelling, you are poised to create content that becomes an integral part of the next-gen search experience. Just as Sephora and Pinterest have embraced this shift, your path to content mastery is one of exploration, innovation, and perpetual evolution, forging a future where content isn't just discovered, but deeply experienced.

Chapter 4

Challenges on the Horizon for SEOs

4.1   E-E-A-T (Experience, Expertise, Authoritativeness, Trustworthiness)

E-E-A-T stands for Experience, Expertise, Authoritativeness, and Trustworthiness. It is a set of criteria that Google uses to evaluate the quality and credibility of websites and online content. Websites that demonstrate high levels of E-E-A-T are more likely to rank higher in search results.

What does E-E-A-T mean?

Experience

This refers to the knowledge and skills that the creators of the content have on the topic they are writing about. It can be demonstrated through things like education, training, and experience.

Expertise

This refers to the depth and breadth of knowledge that the creators of the content have on the topic they are writing about. It can be demonstrated through things like the quality of the content, the use of citations, and the ability to answer complex questions.

Authoritativeness

This refers to the reputation and credibility of the creators of the content. It can be demonstrated through things like the reputation of the website, the number of backlinks, and the presence of awards and accolades.

Trustworthiness

This refers to the confidence that users have in the accuracy and reliability of the content. It can be demonstrated through things like the use of clear and concise language, the absence of bias, and the willingness to disclose conflicts of interest.

What are the challenges of E-E-A-T?

There are several challenges associated with building E-E-A-T for a website or online shop. These challenges include:

Demonstrating experience

It can be difficult to demonstrate experience, especially if you are a new business or website. One way to do this is to cite your sources and provide links to other authoritative content. You can also highlight the qualifications of your team members and the experience they have in the industry.

Establishing expertise

Expertise takes time and effort to develop. You can establish expertise by publishing high-quality content, sharing your knowledge on social media, and speaking at industry events. You can also seek out opportunities to collaborate with other experts in your field.

Building authority

Authority takes time and consistent effort to build. You can build authority by creating backlinks to your website from other high-quality websites. You can also participate in online communities and forums and contribute to other websites and blogs.

Gaining trust

Trust is earned over time. You can gain trust by being transparent about your business practices, providing accurate and reliable information, and resolving any customer issues quickly and effectively.

How important is E-E-A-T for websites and online shops?

E-E-A-T is important for all websites and online shops, but it is especially important for websites that deal with topics that are important to people's lives, such as health, finance, and legal matters. Websites that demonstrate high levels of E-E-A-T are more likely to be trusted by users, and they are more likely to rank higher in search results.

How to improve E-E-A-T for your website or online shop?

There are several things you can do to improve E-E-A-T for your website or online shop. These include:

Create high-quality content

Your content should be well-written, informative, and accurate. It should also be relevant to your target audience.

Use citations

When you cite your sources, you are demonstrating that you have done your research and that you are not just making things up.

Be transparent

Be transparent about your business practices and your qualifications. Let users know who you are and why they can trust you.

Resolve customer issues quickly

When a customer has a problem, resolve it quickly and effectively. This will show users that you are trustworthy and that you care about their satisfaction.

Participate in online communities

Participate in online communities and forums related to your industry. This will help you build relationships with other experts and establish yourself as an authority in your field.

Build backlinks

Build backlinks to your website from other high-quality websites. This will help to improve your website's authority.

By following these tips, you can improve E-E-A-T for your website or online shop and increase your chances of success.

Unpacking E-E-A-T's Significance

E-E-A-T is a critical factor in Google's ranking algorithm, especially for websites that deal with topics that are important to people's lives, such as health, finance, and legal matters. Websites that demonstrate high levels of E-E-A-T are more likely to be trusted by users, and they are more likely to rank higher in search results.

First, it helps Google to determine whether a website is a reliable source of information. Google wants to provide its users with the most accurate and up-to-date information possible, and it uses E-E-A-T to assess the quality of a website's content.

Second, E-E-A-T helps Google to understand the intent of the user. When a user searches for a particular topic, Google wants to return results that are relevant to the user's intent. E-E-A-T helps Google to do this by assessing the expertise of the website's creators and the quality of the content.

Third, E-E-A-T helps Google to combat misinformation. In recent years, there has been a growing problem with misinformation online. Google wants to help its users to identify reliable sources of information, and E-E- A-T is one way that Google does this.

So, how can you improve your website's E-E-A-T?

Create high-quality content:

Your content should be well-written, informative, and accurate. It should also be relevant to your target audience.

Use citations:

When you cite your sources, you are demonstrating that you have done your research and that you are not just making things up.

Be transparent:

Be transparent about your business practices and your qualifications. Let users know who you are and why they can trust you.

Resolve customer issues quickly:

When a customer has a problem, resolve it quickly and effectively. This will show users that you are trustworthy and that you care about their satisfaction.

Participate in online communities:

Participate in online communities and forums related to your industry. This will help you build relationships with other experts and establish yourself as an authority in your field.

Build backlinks:

Build backlinks to your website from other high-quality websites. This will help to improve your website's authority.

By following these tips, you can improve your website's E-E-A-T and increase your chances of success.

Establishing Brand Authority and Trust: Forging Trust and Authority through E-E-A-T

In digital marketing, the principles of E-E-A-T (Expertise, Authoritativeness, Trustworthiness) stand as pillars that not only shape brand perception but also carve a path towards establishing enduring authority and trust. As a digital marketing virtuoso seeking to delve deeper, immersing into the essence of E-E-A-T unveils a world where expertise, authenticity, and reputation intertwine to forge connections that resonate deeply. This chapter embarks on a profound exploration of E-E-A-T, dissecting its facets, deciphering its impact, and providing insights to master this critical aspect of brand authority and trust.

Building Brand Authority

Content Excellence

Create high-quality, well-researched content that showcases expertise, resonates with the target audience, and provides genuine value.

Thought Leadership

Publish thought-provoking insights, industry analysis, and expert opinions that position the brand as a trusted source of information.

Establishing Trust

Authenticity in Brand Voice

Communicate transparently and authentically, allowing users to connect with the human side of the brand.

Credible Backing

Showcase affiliations, partnerships, and endorsements from reputable organizations that validate the brand's authority.

Exemplifying E-E-A-T in Action

Mayo Clinic

The Mayo Clinic's medical expertise, authoritative content, and reputation for accuracy establish it as a trustworthy health resource.

Neil Patel

Neil Patel's marketing insights and contributions across platforms cement his position as an authoritative voice in the digital marketing domain.

Navigating Challenges and Opportunities

Content Consistency

Ensuring uniform expertise and voice across all brand content and channels presents a challenge but solidifies brand authority.

User Reviews and Feedback

Managing online reviews and addressing feedback transparently showcases trustworthiness and willingness to improve.

Crafting an E-E-A-T Focused Strategy

Expert Collaborations

Collaborate with industry experts through guest posts, interviews, and joint initiatives to infuse external authority.

Transparent About Us

Provide detailed information about the brand's history, leadership, and values to bolster trustworthiness.

Future of E-E-A-T

AI and E-E-A-T

As AI evolves, it can analyze content for E-E-A-T attributes, making credibility assessment more efficient and accurate.

User-Centric E-E-A-T

Future E-E-A-T considerations might include the alignment of brand values with user values, ensuring a more empathetic approach.

Conclusion: E-E-A-T as the Cornerstone of Brand Eminence

Diving into the realm of E-E-A-T uncovers a landscape where expertise, authoritativeness, and trustworthiness interlace to establish brand authority and credibility that withstands the tests of time. Your role is that of a conductor orchestrating the harmonious integration of these qualities into every facet of your brand's digital presence. By weaving expert narratives, fostering transparent relationships, and embodying authenticity, you lay the foundation for enduring connections that resonate on the axis of authority and trust. Just as Mayo Clinic and Neil Patel have harnessed E-E-A-T to become industry benchmarks, your journey towards E-E-A- T mastery propels your brand into a future where credibility is not just earned but etched into the very fabric of your brand's identity.

4.2 Aligning E-E-A-T with SEO Practices: Forging a Symbiotic Union

In the dynamic landscape of digital marketing, the harmonious convergence of E-E-A-T (Expertise, Authoritativeness, Trustworthiness) and SEO (Search Engine Optimization) forms a strategic alliance that not only elevates brand visibility but also solidifies credibility in the eyes of search engines and users alike. As a digital marketing virtuoso seeking profound insights, delving into the intricacies of aligning E-E-A-T with SEO practices unveils a world where optimization and authenticity intertwine to craft a digital presence that resonates deeply. This chapter embarks on a comprehensive exploration, deciphering the mechanics, unveiling the strategies, and providing a roadmap to master the synergy between E-E-A-T and SEO for amplified digital impact.

Mechanics of E-E-A-T and SEO Synergy

Expertise in Content Creation

Crafting expert-driven content that showcases subject matter mastery inherently aligns with Google's quality guidelines.

Authoritativeness and Backlinks

Securing authoritative backlinks from reputable sources reinforces the brand's standing as a reliable source of information.

Trustworthiness and User Experience

A transparent, user-focused website design, along with clear privacy and security measures, fosters user trust.

Strategies for Seamless Integration

Keyword Intent Alignment

Optimize content for keywords that align with user intent, ensuring that the brand's expertise is showcased in relevant searches.

Content Diversity

Develop a diverse content portfolio that encompasses authoritative articles, guides, whitepapers, and multimedia content.

Technical SEO and User Experience

Streamlined site navigation, quick loading times, and mobile responsiveness enhance the overall user experience and trustworthiness.

E-E-A-T's Impact on Page Ranking

Content Relevance

Google's algorithms prioritize content that aligns with user intent and demonstrates expertise, often leading to higher rankings.

User Engagement Metrics

Low bounce rates, longer time on site, and high click-through rates validate content quality and authoritative positioning.

Exemplifying E-E-A-T and SEO Success

WebMD

The medical expertise, authoritative content, and user trust associated with WebMD translate into strong search visibility.

Wikipedia

Wikipedia's authority and trustworthy information often lead to top-ranking positions, exemplifying E-E-A-T's impact.

Futureproofing with E-E-A-T and SEO

Voice Search and E-E-A-T

As voice search gains prominence, aligning content with E-E-A-T attributes enhances visibility in conversational searches.

Algorithm Evolution

Search algorithms continue to evolve, focusing on content credibility and user satisfaction, making E-E-A-T a lasting factor.

Conclusion: Orchestrating E-E-A-T and SEO Harmony for unparalleled Impact

As you navigate the synergy between E-E-A-T and SEO, you uncover a realm where optimization transcends mere algorithms, resonating deeply with user needs and search engine requirements alike. Your role as a digital marketing visionary is that of a conductor harmonizing content quality, relevance, and authenticity to create a symphony of expertise, authority, and trust. By aligning keyword strategies with user intent, fostering transparent relationships, and ensuring an exceptional user experience, you chart a course toward digital prominence that not only captures search engine attention but also secures user trust. Just as WebMD and Wikipedia have harnessed this synergy, your journey towards E-E-A-T and SEO mastery propels your brand into a future where credibility and visibility intertwine, creating a lasting impact that resonates through the digital corridors.

4.3 Future SEO Challenges and Solutions

Navigating Evolving Search Algorithms: Unveiling Solutions for a Dynamic Digital Landscape

In the intricate labyrinth of evolving search algorithms, solutions emerge as guiding beacons to navigate the unpredictable currents of change with finesse and strategic prowess. As a digital marketing trailblazer poised on the precipice of transformation, delving into the depths of these solutions unveils a landscape where adaptability, resilience, and innovation converge. This chapter embarks on a profound exploration, dissecting challenges, illuminating strategies, and unveiling concrete solutions that empower you to not only weather algorithmic storms but to thrive amidst them.

Solution 1: Embrace User-Centricity and Quality

Content Relevance and Quality:

Prioritize creating in-depth, valuable content that addresses users' needs, fostering engagement and user satisfaction.

E-E-A-T Compliance:

Bolster Expertise, Authoritativeness, and Trustworthiness attributes to resonate with evolving algorithms that prioritize user trust.

Solution 2: Strategic Data-Driven Insights

Algorithm Monitoring:

Stay vigilant by using tools to monitor algorithmic updates and trends, adapting strategies in real-time.

User Behavior Analysis:

Analyze user behavior data to understand how algorithms impact user interactions, optimizing content accordingly.

Solution 3: Technical Optimization Mastery

Mobile Responsiveness:

Ensure your website is mobile-friendly to align with algorithms' mobile- first indexing and enhance user experiences.

Page Speed Optimization:

Optimize loading times to cater to algorithms' preference for fast, user-friendly websites.

Solution 4: Adaptive SEO Techniques

Semantic Keyword Targeting:

Focus on context and user intent rather than exact keywords to align with algorithms' language understanding.

Structured Data Markup:

Utilize schema markup to provide context to search engines, enhancing the visibility of content features like snippets and rich results.

Solution 5: Amplify User Engagement

User-Centric Design:

Create intuitive, user-friendly website navigation that encourages longer time on site and lower bounce rates.

Interactive Elements:

Employ multimedia content, quizzes, and surveys to drive user engagement and interaction.

Solution 6: AI-Enhanced Optimization

AI-Driven Insights:

Leverage AI tools to analyze large datasets, gain insights into user preferences, and adapt strategies accordingly.

Predictive Analytics:

Utilize AI for predictive analysis, anticipating user behavior trends and algorithmic shifts.

Solution 7: Holistic Brand Reputation Management

Online Reputation Management

Manage online reviews, feedback, and discussions to build and maintain a positive brand reputation.

Expert Collaborations

Collaborate with industry experts to enhance your brand's authority and credibility, aligning with algorithms' focus on E-E-A-T.

Solution 8: Cultivate Adaptive Agility

Agile Mindset

Foster a culture of adaptability within your team, encouraging quick responses to algorithmic changes.

Constant Learning

Invest in continuous learning and stay updated with digital marketing trends and algorithmic shifts.

Conclusion: Mastering Algorithmic Evolution with Strategic Solutions

As you navigate the intricate terrain of evolving search algorithms, solutions become the cornerstone of your digital marketing strategy. Your role as a digital marketing visionary is that of an architect, building strategies that harmonize with algorithmic changes, user preferences, and your brand's unique identity. By embracing user-centricity, leveraging data insights, and mastering technical optimization, you wield the tools needed to thrive amidst the dynamic currents of change. Just as successful brands have adapted their SEO techniques, optimized for mobile experiences, and embraced AI-enhanced strategies, your journey towards algorithmic mastery is one of resilience, innovation, and perpetual evolution, ensuring that your brand not only survives but thrives in the ever-shifting landscape of digital marketing.

4.4   Mobile-First and Voice Search Optimization

Unveiling the Mobile-First and Voice Search Revolution

In the dynamic realm of digital marketing, the convergence of mobile- first and voice search optimization forms a transformative juncture that demands a reimagining of strategies for brands across all levels. As a digital marketing sage poised on the precipice of innovation, delving into the intricacies of mobile-first and voice search optimization unveils a landscape where convenience, context, and creativity intertwine. This chapter embarks on an immersive exploration, dissecting challenges, unveiling possibilities, and providing innovative strategies to master the art of mobile-first and voice search optimization that resonates with users of all levels.

Mobile-First Optimization: Challenges and Strategies

Responsive Design

Crafting responsive websites that seamlessly adapt to various screen sizes presents a challenge but enhances user experience.

Loading Speed

Ensuring swift loading times, particularly on mobile devices, is crucial for both user satisfaction and search ranking.

Unlocking Mobile-First Possibilities

Accelerated Mobile Pages (AMP)

Creating AMP versions of content enhances page speed, providing a smoother mobile experience.

Mobile-Friendly UI/UX

Crafting user-friendly interfaces, intuitive navigation, and thumb-friendly design enhances mobile engagement.

Voice Search Optimization: Challenges and Strategies

Natural Language Queries

Voice search revolves around conversational queries, demanding a shift from keyword-focused content.

Local Context

Users often employ voice search for local queries, necessitating location specific optimization strategies.

Embracing Voice Search's Potential

Featured Snippets

Creating concise, informative answers to common queries increases the chances of being featured as a voice search result.

Structured Data Markup

Employing schema markup helps search engines understand and present information in voice search results.

Seamless Integration of Mobile-First and Voice Optimization

Contextual Keyword Research

Focus on conversational keywords that align with voice queries while considering mobile user intent.

Local SEO and Voice Search

Optimize for local searches, catering to both mobile users on the go and voice searchers seeking nearby solutions.

Innovative Solutions for Accessibility

Voice Navigation

Implement voice navigation options for users who require hands-free browsing, ensuring inclusivity.

Visual and Auditory Content Fusion

Blend visuals and audio to cater to diverse sensory experiences for users of all levels.

Personalized Experiences and User Behavior

User Behavior Insights

Analyze user interactions to understand how mobile and voice users navigate content differently.

Location-Based Personalization

Customize content based on users' locations for tailored mobile-first and voice experiences.

The Future of Mobile-First and Voice Optimization

AI-Driven Personalization

AI advancements will allow for more accurate predictions of user behavior, tailoring content accordingly.

Device-agnostic Experiences

As technology evolves, crafting experiences that are seamless across devices will become paramount.

Conclusion: Forging Ahead in the Mobile-First and Voice Search Epoch

As you navigate the crossroads of mobile-first and voice search optimization, you embark on a journey that unifies convenience, context, and innovation. Your role as a digital marketing visionary is that of a conductor orchestrating strategies that resonate with users across all levels, devices, and preferences. By embracing responsive design, harnessing voice-friendly content, and fostering personalized experiences, you forge a path that not only enhances brand visibility but also cultivates user loyalty. Just as brands have optimized for mobile-first experiences and embraced voice-friendly content, your journey towards mobile-first and voice optimization mastery propels your brand into a future where accessibility, convenience, and creativity harmonize to create a digital presence that resonates with users of all levels.

4.5 Data Privacy and Ethical SEO Practices

Safeguarding Trust: Data Privacy and Ethical SEO Practices in the Digital Landscape

In the intricate web of digital marketing, the preservation of data privacy and the adherence to ethical SEO practices stand as pivotal pillars that not only shape brand integrity but also cultivate lasting trust among audiences across all levels. As a digital marketing guardian on the path of ethical excellence, immersing into the complexities of data privacy and ethical SEO practices unveils a realm where transparency, respect, and responsibility converge. This chapter embarks on a profound exploration, dissecting challenges, unveiling strategies, and providing insights to navigate the terrain of data privacy and ethical SEO, ensuring a digital presence that resonates ethically with users of all levels.

Data Privacy Challenges and Strategies

User Consent

Balancing personalized experiences with user consent demands clear communication and user-friendly opt-in processes.

Transparency

Communicating data collection methods and usage to users builds trust and fosters a sense of control.

Upholding Data Privacy Possibilities

Cookie Consent

Implementing user-friendly cookie consent banners respects user choices regarding data collection.

Data Protection Measures

Utilizing encryption and secure protocols safeguards user data against breaches and unauthorized access.

Ethical SEO Practices: Challenges and Strategies

Black Hat Tactics

Resisting the allure of shortcuts like keyword stuffing and cloaking ensures a sustainable, ethical SEO approach.

Content Authenticity

Prioritizing original, valuable content over duplicate or spun content establishes brand integrity.

Fostering Ethical SEO Excellence

Keyword Research Balance

Target keywords with relevance and user intent, avoiding manipulative tactics that undermine authenticity.

Link Building Integrity

Focus on quality over quantity when building backlinks, avoiding link schemes that compromise credibility.

Synthesis of Data Privacy and Ethical SEO

Privacy-Centric SEO Strategy

Craft SEO strategies that consider user data protection, incorporating ethical practices into your optimization efforts.

Transparency in Tracking

Clearly communicate data tracking practices and offer opt-out mechanisms for users who prioritize privacy.

Striking the Balance for User Trust

Educational Resources

Develop content that educates users about data privacy, fostering trust through transparency.

Ethical Brand Positioning

Champion your brand's ethical stance on data privacy and responsible SEO practices to build credibility.

Ethical SEO's Future Horizons

Algorithmic Considerations

Search algorithms may evolve to prioritize ethical practices, rewarding brands that prioritize user well-being.

Legislative Impact

Growing privacy regulations may necessitate more stringent data protection practices in SEO strategies.

Conclusion: Forging Ethical Eminence in a Data-Driven Era

As you navigate the intricate landscape of data privacy and ethical SEO practices, you step into a realm where user trust is the cornerstone of digital success. Your role as a digital marketing guardian is to be an ethical compass, guiding strategies that resonate with users' values, respecting their data, and fostering transparency. By prioritizing user consent, embracing authenticity, and cultivating ethical SEO practices, you weave a narrative of trust and integrity that extends beyond algorithms. Just as brands have aligned with data protection regulations and prioritized ethical content, your journey towards ethical SEO mastery propels your brand into a future where data privacy and ethical practices harmonize to create a digital presence that resonates ethically and reverberates trust across all levels of users.

Chapter 5

Multimedia's Dominance in Digital Marketing

5.1 Embracing the Multifaceted Canvas: Multimedia's Dominance in Digital Marketing

In the kaleidoscopic landscape of digital marketing, a new era is dawning—one defined by the captivating fusion of visual, auditory, and interactive elements that weaves a tapestry of engagement like never before. Welcome to a world where multimedia's dominance reigns supreme, transforming the way brands communicate, connect, and captivate audiences across the digital spectrum. As we embark on this exploration, prepare to journey through a realm where images, videos, animations, and interactive experiences converge, offering a panoramic view of how multimedia has evolved from an enhancement to an indispensable cornerstone of digital marketing strategies.

Gone are the days when text alone held sway; today, the attention economy is shaped by the alchemy of captivating visuals, resonant sounds, and immersive interactions. As we delve deeper, we'll navigate the reasons behind multimedia's ascendancy, uncover the strategies that underpin its effectiveness, and examine the ways it invigorates branding, storytelling, and user engagement. The digital landscape now orbits around the sun of multimedia, inviting brands of all sizes and industries to harness its limitless potential and elevate their marketing endeavors to unprecedented heights.

This chapter invites you to embark on a journey through the expansive universe of multimedia in digital marketing. Together, we'll traverse its power to captivate, communicate, and convey complex narratives; explore its role in fostering deeper connections with diverse audiences; and unveil the innovative strategies that marry creativity and technology to forge an unforgettable user experience. As a digital marketing visionary, prepare to unlock the secrets to welding multimedia's magic as you navigate the intricacies of visual storytelling, harness the resonance of sound, and pioneer interactive journeys that leave an indelible imprint on the hearts and minds of consumers.

With multimedia as our guiding star, we invite you to join us on this expedition—one that delves into the heart of creativity, embraces the symphony of senses, and unfurls the possibilities that lie at the intersection of innovation and engagement. So, buckle up and immerse yourself in the compelling odyssey of multimedia's dominance in the digital marketing cosmos.

5.2   Power of Video Content

The Cinematic Revolution: Unveiling the Profound Power of Video Content

In the dynamic arena of digital marketing, video content emerges as a towering titan, poised to reshape the very foundations of engagement, communication, and storytelling. Prepare to embark on a deep dive into the captivating realm of video, understanding why its allure is destined to shape the future of marketing and how its versatile prowess can be harnessed within a strategic multichannel approach.

The Ascendance of Video

Visual Dominance

The human brain processes visuals 60,000 times faster than text, making videos a natural preference for consumption.

Emotional Resonance

Videos evoke emotions through visuals, sounds, and storytelling, forging connections that resonate deeply with audiences.

Unraveling Video's Importance

Engagement Magnet

Video content captures attention, leading to longer on-page times, reduced bounce rates, and heightened engagement.

Storytelling Amplification

Through moving images and audio, videos enhance narrative delivery, making brand stories more compelling.

Future Foresight: Why Videos Are Essential

Rise of Video-First Platforms

Social media platforms prioritize video, indicating a future where video content is paramount.

Augmented Reality Integration

As AR evolves, videos will enable immersive experiences, combining the real world with virtual elements.

Multichannel Strategy: The Art of Video Integration

Social Media Symphony

Adapt video content for different platforms, leveraging each channel's unique features and audience behavior.

Email Engagement

Embed videos in emails to increase click-through rates, offering dynamic content directly in users' inboxes.

Video SEO Mastery

Keyword Optimization

Use relevant keywords in video titles, descriptions, and tags to improve search visibility on platforms like YouTube.

Transcriptions and Subtitles

Enhance accessibility and SEO by providing transcriptions and subtitles for video content.

Interactive Videos: Engaging the Viewer

Choose-Your-Own-Adventure

Interactive videos allow viewers to make choices, creating personalized journeys that enhance engagement.

360-Degree Immersion

Immerse viewers in virtual environments, enabling them to explore and interact with the content.

Embracing Live Streaming: Real-Time Connection

Authenticity Appeal

Live streaming fosters real-time interactions, allowing brands to connect with audiences in authentic ways.

Event Broadcasting

Live streaming events, product launches, and Q&A sessions build anticipation and engagement.

User-Generated Content and Video

Harnessing Advocacy

Encourage users to create video testimonials, reviews, and content, leveraging their genuine enthusiasm.

Crowdsourced Creativity

Invite users to contribute videos that showcase their experiences, creating a sense of community.

The Power of Emotional Appeal

Showcasing Humanity

Videos humanize brands by showcasing their people, values, and behind- the-scenes moments.

Tapping into Empathy

Emotional narratives create connections, encouraging viewers to support brands they resonate with.

Conclusion: Crafting a Video Symphony Across Channels

As we delve into the depths of video's might, it's evident that this dynamic medium is poised to be the driving force behind future marketing landscapes. Your role as a digital marketing visionary is that of a director, orchestrating a cinematic experience that resonates across channels, platforms, and devices. By integrating videos strategically, personalizing experiences, and tapping into the emotive power of visuals and sound, you create an immersive journey that captivates, educates, and engages audiences with lasting impact. Just as brands have harnessed the potential of video content across platforms and mediums, your journey towards mastering video's power propels your brand into a future where engagement is not just a metric but an emotional connection, seamlessly woven into the fabric of your multichannel marketing tapestry.

5.3 Rise of Video Content Consumption

The Unstoppable Ascension: Chronicles of the Rise of Video Content Consumption

Amid the ever-evolving tapestry of digital marketing, an epochal shift has taken place—a seismic rise in the consumption of video content, shaping the narrative of engagement, connection, and communication. Let us embark on a journey through time, tracing the remarkable trajectory of video content consumption, from its modest beginnings to its current pedestal, and envisioning its role as a pivotal force in shaping the future of how brands connect with their audiences.

The Genesis: Birth of a Visual Revolution

In the early days, video content was a rarity—bandwidth limitations and technical constraints made its adoption a challenge. Yet, pioneers recognized its potential to convey messages, share stories, and immerse viewers in a world of moving images and sound.

The YouTube Revolution: A Catalyst for Change

The dawn of YouTube brought forth a democratization of content creation and consumption. Individuals and brands alike flocked to this platform, unlocking the power of video for sharing everything from educational content to entertainment spectacles.

The Mobile Era: A Game-Changer for Accessibility

As smartphones became ubiquitous, video consumption underwent a transformation. Pocket-sized screens offered the promise of content anytime, anywhere, redefining how users engaged with brands and narratives.

Visual Storytelling: Eliciting Emotions and Connections

The rise of video content wasn't just about information dissemination; it was a profound shift towards emotional resonance. Brands discovered that videos could weave narratives that touched hearts, fostering connections that transcended mere transactions.

Social Media: The Power of Virality and Sharing

Social media platforms became the launchpads for viral sensations and cultural phenomena. The sharing culture propelled videos to unprecedented reach, igniting conversations, trends, and movements.

Live Streaming: Authenticity in Real-Time

The advent of live streaming introduced a new dimension of authenticity. Brands connected with audiences in real-time, unveiling unscripted moments and fostering a sense of inclusivity.

Video-First Platforms: The Dawn of a New Era

The rise of platforms like TikTok and Instagram Reels heralded a video- first era, catering to shorter attention spans and capitalizing on the art of concise storytelling.

Educational Renaissance: Learning Through Videos

Beyond entertainment, videos became a go-to source for learning. Tutorials, webinars, and educational content flourished, transforming the way individuals acquired new skills and knowledge.

The Future Envisioned: Video as the Lingua Franca

As we gaze into the future, it's evident that video content consumption will continue to ascend. From virtual reality to augmented reality, from interactive narratives to personalized experiences, the possibilities are boundless.

Conclusion: The Odyssey Continues: The Tapestry of Video Content Consumption

As we trace the trajectory of video content consumption, we recognize that it's more than a trend—it's an evolutionary phenomenon that shapes how we perceive, interact, and engage with the world around us. Your role as a digital marketing storyteller is to harness the power of this medium, crafting narratives that capture hearts, ignite imaginations, and forge connections that transcend screens. Just as brands have adapted to the rise of video consumption, your journey towards mastery embraces the art of visual storytelling, fostering authentic connections that navigate the currents of change and inspire a future where video content reigns as the bridge between brands and their audiences.

5.4 Tapping into Emotional and Visual Appeal: Navigating Challenges, Unveiling Possibilities

In the tapestry of digital marketing, the threads of emotion and visual allure are intricately woven, creating a canvas that captures attention, resonates deeply, and fosters connections beyond the transactional. Prepare to journey deeper into the heart of this symbiotic relationship, where challenges are met with innovative strategies and where the power of emotional and visual appeal is harnessed to craft content that lingers in the minds and hearts of audiences.

Challenges: Unveiling the Landscape of Emotion and Visuals

Balancing Authenticity

Striking the right balance between emotional engagement and authentic representation can be complex, requiring finesse and transparency.

Cultural Sensitivity

The global audience demands sensitivity to diverse cultural nuances, ensuring that emotions and visuals resonate universally.

Possibilities: Crafting Compelling Emotional Narratives

Empathy-Driven Content

Use stories that evoke empathy, allowing audiences to see themselves in the narrative and forming deeper connections.

Humanizing the Brand

Showcase real people and human experiences, grounding the brand in relatability and authenticity.

Challenges: Harnessing Visual Appeal's Potential

Information Overload

In a visually saturated world, breaking through the noise demands innovative visual elements that capture attention swiftly.

Consistency

Maintaining a cohesive visual identity across diverse platforms can be challenging, ensuring that audiences instantly recognize the brand.

Possibilities: Crafting Visually Arresting Content

Visual Consistency

Establish a visual brand identity with consistent colors, fonts, and design elements, ensuring instant recognition.

Visual Storytelling

Use visuals to tell stories that transcend language barriers, leaving a lasting imprint on the audience's memory.

Challenges: Balancing Emotional Depth and Visual Aesthetics

Message Clarity

Balancing emotional depth with the clarity of the message can sometimes lead to information getting lost amidst the sentiment.

Overarching Theme

Ensuring that visuals and emotions align with the brand's overarching theme and values can be intricate.

Possibilities: Crafting the Perfect Synthesis

Narrative Alignment

Ensure that the emotional narrative aligns seamlessly with the visual aesthetics, creating a harmonious and impactful experience.

Call to Action

Drive emotions towards a clear call to action, guiding audiences on the next steps they can take with the brand.

Challenges: Measuring Emotional Impact and Visual Resonance

Quantifying Emotions

Measuring emotional impact can be challenging, as emotions are subjective and may vary from person to person.

Visual Engagement Metrics

Identifying metrics that accurately measure visual engagement beyond mere views can be complex.

Possibilities: Analyzing Emotional and Visual Metrics

User Feedback

Solicit feedback directly from the audience to gauge emotional resonance and visual impact.

Time-on-Visual Metrics

Look beyond mere views to metrics like time spent engaging with visuals to assess their true impact.

Conclusion: Mastering the Art of Emotion and Visuals

As you navigate the intricate interplay between emotion and visual allure, you embrace a realm where stories become connections, and visuals become the language of engagement. Your role as a digital marketing artisan is to create a symphony that resonates with authenticity, captures attention through visual ingenuity, and leaves an indelible emotional mark. Just as brands have tapped into the fusion of emotion and visuals, your journey towards mastery marries creativity with strategy, ensuring that your content isn't just consumed—it's felt and remembered, echoing through the minds of your audience, fostering a future where every engagement is a meaningful, emotional, and visually captivating experience.

5.5 Crafting a Comprehensive Strategy

Navigating the Labyrinth of Digital Marketing Mastery

In the vast expanse of digital marketing, a comprehensive strategy stands as the North Star—a guiding constellation that illuminates the path to success, ensuring every action resonates with purpose and every engagement echoes with impact. Prepare to embark on a profound expedition into the heart of crafting a comprehensive strategy, where every layer is peeled back, every facet is explored, and every nuance is dissected from a digital marketing perspective.

Foundation: Aligning with Business Objectives

Business Goals Integration

Anchor your strategy to the core business objectives, ensuring every effort advances the organization's mission.

Audience Persona Mapping

Create detailed audience personas, diving deep into demographics, preferences, behaviors, and pain points.

Embrace the Digital Ecosystem

Channel Diversity

Understand the strengths and nuances of each digital channel, from social media to SEO, tailoring strategies for maximum impact.

Multichannel Cohesion

Ensure seamless integration across channels, crafting a unified brand experience that resonates at every touchpoint.

Content Creation and Distribution

Content Mapping

Map content to each stage of the buyer's journey, from awareness to conversion, nurturing prospects along the way.

Value-Driven Content

Craft content that offers value, answers questions, and addresses pain points, positioning your brand as a trusted resource.

Data-Driven Decision Making

Analytics Implementation

Set up robust analytics tools to track key metrics, enabling data-driven adjustments and optimizations.

Conversion Funnel Analysis

Deep dive into the conversion funnel, identifying drop-off points and optimizing each stage for maximum efficiency.

Personalization for Engagement

Segmentation Strategy

Segment your audience based on behavior, preferences, and demographics to deliver hyper-personalized experiences.

Dynamic Content

Leverage dynamic content that adapts to user interactions, providing tailored experiences that foster engagement.

Search Engine Optimization (SEO) Mastery

Keyword Strategy

Research and target relevant keywords to ensure your content ranks high in search engine results.

Technical SEO

Optimize website speed, mobile-friendliness, and user experience for optimal search performance.

Social Media Amplification

Platform Selection

Choose social platforms aligned with your audience and goals, tailoring content formats to each platform's strengths.

Community Building

Foster genuine interactions with your audience, creating a community that engages with your brand organically.

Paid Advertising Precision

Audience Targeting

Refine your audience targeting based on demographics, interests, and behaviors to maximize ad relevance.

A/B Testing

Conduct A/B tests to optimize ad creatives, copy, and landing pages for higher conversion rates.

Email Marketing Excellence

Segmented Campaigns

Create segmented email lists for targeted campaigns, delivering content that resonates with specific segments.

Automation Efficiency

Implement marketing automation to nurture leads, drive engagement, and optimize customer journeys.

Conversion Rate Optimization (CRO)

Landing Page Optimization

Craft compelling landing pages with clear calls to action and persuasive elements for higher conversions.

User Experience Enhancement

Continuously improve user experience to reduce friction and encourage seamless conversions.

Innovative Technology Integration

AI and Machine Learning

Embrace AI for predictive analytics, personalization, and dynamic content creation.

Virtual Reality (VR) and Augmented Reality (AR)

Explore VR and AR to provide immersive experiences that stand out in the digital landscape.

Conclusion: Orchestrating a Masterpiece of Strategy

Your role is that of a conductor, blending creativity and strategy into a harmonious symphony of engagement. By aligning with business objectives, leveraging the digital ecosystem, crafting compelling content, and embracing data-driven insights, you forge a comprehensive strategy that transcends conventional tactics. Just as brands have honed their digital strategies, your journey towards mastery embodies the fusion of art and science, forging a future where every digital interaction is a symphony of purpose, impact, and resonance.

5.6 The Unified Approach to Digital Marketing: Weaving Threads of Excellence into a Singular Strategy

In the intricate realm of digital marketing, a unified approach emerges as the ultimate tapestry—a masterpiece woven from threads of cohesion, synergy, and strategic alignment. Prepare to delve into the depths of the unified approach, where every element is meticulously orchestrated to resonate with a singular purpose, harmonizing channels, strategies, and efforts into a symphony of excellence that resonates with audiences and propels brands to unprecedented heights.

Foundation: The Core Tenets of Unity

Strategic Clarity

Define a clear and cohesive strategy that aligns with overarching business goals, guiding every action with purpose.

Cross-Channel Integration

Seamlessly integrate various digital channels, ensuring consistent messaging, branding, and user experience.

Synergy Across Channels

Omnichannel Strategy

Develop a strategy that traverses diverse digital channels, bridging touchpoints for a cohesive user journey.

Consistent Messaging

Craft a unified brand message that resonates across channels, reinforcing brand identity and values.

Content Harmonization

Content Alignment

Align content creation with audience needs, ensuring that each piece contributes to the overall narrative.

Repurposing Strategy

Repurpose content across channels, adapting it to suit different formats and platforms while maintaining its core essence.

Data-Driven Insights

Data Integration

Integrate data from various sources to gain a holistic view of audience behaviors, preferences, and engagement patterns.

Holistic Analysis

Analyze data to uncover cross-channel insights, identifying trends that inform strategies across the entire spectrum.

Personalization Across Channels

Cross-Channel Personalization

Utilize data-driven insights to deliver personalized experiences seamlessly across channels.

Unified Customer Profiles

Develop unified customer profiles that capture interactions and preferences across all touchpoints.

Paid and Organic Symbiosis

Paid and Organic Alignment

Align paid advertising and organic efforts, ensuring consistent messaging and optimized user journeys.

Leveraging Insights

Use insights from paid campaigns to refine organic strategies, and vice versa, creating a feedback loop of optimization.

Unified Brand Voice

Voice and Tone Consistency

Maintain a consistent brand voice and tone across all interactions, building recognition and trust.

Cohesive Visual Identity

Harmonize visual elements like logos, colors, and design aesthetics across all channels and materials.

Customer-Centric Engagement

Customer Journey Mapping

Map the customer journey across channels, identifying touchpoints for meaningful interactions.

Seamless Transition

Ensure a seamless transition as customers move between channels, fostering a fluid and engaging experience.

Innovative Technology Integration

Unified Technology Stack

Integrate tools and platforms to streamline workflows and data sharing across teams and channels.

AI-Powered Insights

Leverage AI to analyze data and provide insights that optimize strategies across the unified landscape.

Conclusion: Crafting a Singular Symphony of Success

As you embark on the journey of the unified approach to digital marketing, you become the maestro orchestrating a symphony of synergy, coherence, and effectiveness. Your role is to harmonize channels, synchronize strategies, and resonate with audiences in a way that transcends individual efforts. Just as brands have embraced the unified approach to redefine digital marketing, your journey towards mastery embodies the fusion of strategy and execution, forging a future where every interaction is a note in the symphony of excellence—a symphony that resonates, engages, and inspires, forging a legacy of digital marketing brilliance.

5.7 Synergy of PPC, SEO, and Social Media with Visual Content

The Symbiotic Dance: Unveiling the Synergy of PPC, SEO, Social Media, and Visual Content

In the intricate tapestry of digital marketing, a mesmerizing dance un- folds—a dance that involves the harmonious interplay of Pay-Per-Click (PPC), Search Engine Optimization (SEO), social media, and Visual Content. Prepare to venture into the heart of this captivating choreography, where each element contributes its unique rhythm, weaving a symphony of engagement, visibility, and resonance that captivates audiences and propels brands to new heights.

Foundation: Orchestrating a Unified Vision

Unified Strategy

Craft a comprehensive strategy that aligns PPC, SEO, and social media efforts, forging a cohesive narrative across channels.

Visual Storytelling

Harness the power of visual content to amplify messaging, create emotional connections, and enhance engagement.

PPC, SEO, and Social Media: The Harmonious Trio

PPC Precision

Utilize PPC campaigns to target specific keywords, generate immediate visibility, and drive traffic to targeted landing pages.

SEO Authority

Optimize website content for relevant keywords, elevating organic search rankings and fostering long-term credibility.

Social Media Amplification

Distribute visual content across social platforms, leveraging their virality and engagement potential.

Visual Content: The Visual Thread

Emotional Impact

Visual content creates emotional resonance, enabling audiences to connect deeply with brand stories and messages.

Information Digestion

Visuals convey complex information quickly, enhancing user experience and encouraging exploration.

The User Journey: A Unified Odyssey

Awareness Stage

PPC campaigns drive immediate awareness, while SEO ensures long-term visibility, and social media amplifies reach.

Consideration Stage

Engaging visual content on social media fuels interest, while SEO-optimized content provides in-depth insights.

Conversion Stage

Visual content in PPC ads drives conversions, while SEO positions your brand as a credible solution.

Keyword Synergy

PPC and SEO Collaboration

Insights from PPC campaigns identify high-converting keywords that can be optimized for SEO efforts.

Shared Learning

Data from PPC campaigns informs SEO keyword choices, enhancing organic search strategies.

Amplifying Social Media Engagement

Visual Appeal

Engaging visual content on social platforms enhances engagement, encouraging sharing and interaction.

SEO and Social Signals

High social engagement can positively impact SEO rankings, indicating relevance and user satisfaction.

Unified Analytics: Data-Driven Insights

Cross-Channel Analysis

Analyze data from PPC, SEO, and social media to uncover holistic audience behavior patterns.

Iterative Optimization

Use insights to refine strategies across channels, creating a continuous cycle of improvement.

Conclusion: Crafting a Symphony of Digital Mastery

As you delve into the synergy of PPC, SEO, social media, and visual content, you become the conductor of a grand symphony—a symphony that blends strategy, creativity, and innovation. Your role is to unite these elements into a seamless experience, guiding audiences through a journey that resonates, informs, and inspires. Just as brands have harnessed the power of this harmonious interplay, your journey towards mastery is one of finesse, forging a future where every touchpoint is orchestrated, every message resonates, and every interaction becomes an integral part of the captivating dance that is digital marketing.

5.8 Delivering Consistent Brand Message

Unveiling the Art of Consistency: Delivering a Brand Message That Resonates

In the symphony of digital marketing, a consistent brand message emerges as the powerful melody that lingers in the minds of audiences, shaping perceptions, building trust, and forging lasting connections. Prepare to journey into the heart of this melodic mastery, where every note is strategically orchestrated to resonate across channels, platforms, and touchpoints, creating a harmonious brand narrative that echoes with clarity and purpose.

Foundation: The Core of Cohesion

Defining the Essence

Establish a clear brand identity, including values, mission, voice, and visual elements that form the foundation of your message.

Unified Messaging

Craft a core message that encapsulates your brand's purpose, creating a central theme that threads through all communications.

Strategies for Consistency

Unified Tone and Voice

Maintain a consistent tone that aligns with your brand's personality, ensuring a cohesive voice in all interactions.

Message Hierarchy

Prioritize key messages that need to be conveyed and ensure they are reiterated across various touchpoints.

Omnipresence Across Channels

Website Harmonization

Infuse your website with your brand's voice, visual identity, and messaging for a seamless user experience.

Social Media Congruence

Craft posts, captions, and visuals that consistently reflect your brand's essence, creating a unified presence.

Email Communication Mastery

Subject Line Alignment

Ensure subject lines resonate with your brand, setting expectations for what recipients will find inside.

Content Consistency

Deliver email content that aligns with your brand's narrative, reinforcing its values and messaging.

Visual Identity Reinforcement

Visual Elements

Consistently use brand colors, fonts, and design elements across all visuals to reinforce brand recognition.

Imagery Cohesion

Choose images that reflect your brand's values and evoke the desired emotions, creating a visual story that resonates.

Storytelling Continuity

Narrative Consistency

Weave a cohesive narrative across all content, from blog posts to social media updates, creating a story arc that resonates.

User-Centric Approach

Tailor your brand message to resonate with your audience's aspirations, challenges, and desires, creating relatable content.

Cross-Channel Synergy

PPC and SEO Alignment

Ensure the messaging in your PPC ads aligns with your SEO-optimized content, creating a consistent user journey.

Social Media and Website Fusion

Seamlessly connect your social media content to your website, allowing audiences to transition without dissonance.

Employee Advocacy: Amplifying the Echo

Internal Consistency

Educate your team on the brand's messaging and values, encouraging them to be brand advocates.

Amplified Reach

Empower employees to share your brand message, expanding your reach and authenticity.

Feedback Loop for Refinement

Audience Feedback

Listen to your audience's responses and adapt your message based on their perceptions and reactions.

Continuous Optimization

Continuously refine your messaging strategy based on performance metrics and evolving audience preferences.

Conclusion: The Symphony of Brand Resonance

As you immerse yourself in the art of delivering a consistent brand message, you become the composer of a symphony that resonates across the digital landscape. Your role is to orchestrate a narrative that harmonizes voice, visuals, and values, creating an unforgettable melody that reverberates in the hearts of your audience. Just as brands have mastered the art of consistency, your journey towards mastery involves the fusion of creativity and strategy, forging a future where every interaction is a note in the symphony of brand resonance—a symphony that captivates, connects, and leaves an indelible mark on the canvas of digital marketing.

5.9 Embracing Evolution

The Dynamic Nature of Digital

Acknowledge that the digital realm is a fluid canvas, shaped by emerging technologies, shifting consumer behaviors, and evolving search algorithms.

Continuous Learning

Commit to a culture of lifelong learning, staying abreast of industry trends, algorithm updates, and emerging platforms.

Agile Adaptation

Flexibility as a Virtue

Build flexibility into your strategies, enabling swift pivots when market dynamics demand it.

Test and Iterate

Embrace a test-and-learn mindset, experimenting with new approaches, analyzing results, and refining strategies accordingly.

Technology Integration

AI and Automation

Embrace AI-powered tools and automation to streamline processes, optimize campaigns, and glean data-driven insights.

Predictive Analytics

Leverage predictive analytics to anticipate trends, optimizing your strategy for maximum impact.

Human-Centric Focus

Empathy-Driven Approach

Keep the human element at the forefront of your strategy, understanding and catering to the needs, preferences, and emotions of your audience.

Personalization Continuum

Explore deeper personalization by leveraging data insights to create hyper targeted, relevant experiences.

Sustainable Engagement

Ethical Practices

Uphold ethical SEO, data privacy, and user experience practices to maintain long-term credibility and trust.

Sustainability Initiatives

Incorporate sustainable values and practices into your strategy, aligning with the values of eco-conscious consumers.

Embracing New Platforms

Emerging Platforms

Stay open to embracing new platforms and technologies that resonate with your audience, even if they deviate from traditional strategies.

Cross-Platform Integration

Seamlessly integrate new platforms into your existing strategy, ensuring a unified brand presence.

Staying Ahead of Search Evolution

Algorithmic Agility

Understand that search algorithms will continue to evolve. Stay proactive in adapting your SEO tactics to align with new updates.

Voice and Visual Search

Embrace the rise of voice and visual search, optimizing your content for these emergent search methods.

Investing in Education

Internal Training

Foster a culture of education within your team, encouraging regular skill building and sharing of industry insights.

External Resources

Leverage webinars, conferences, and industry publications to gain insights from experts and stay informed.

Conclusion: Crafting a Visionary Path Forward

As you stand at the intersection of your journey, armed with knowledge, creativity, and strategic prowess, remember that future-proofing your digital marketing strategy is a perpetual voyage. The digital landscape will continue to evolve, and your role as a digital marketing trailblazer is to chart a visionary path that embraces change, anticipates trends, and engages audiences in ways that resonate across channels and time. Just as brands have navigated the waves of digital transformation, your journey towards mastery embraces the fusion of innovation and tradition, propelling you toward a future where your digital marketing strategy stands as a beacon of resilience, relevance, and boundless possibilities.

5.10 Embracing Continuous Adaptation

In this section, we delve into the importance of continuous adaptation in the dynamic landscape of digital marketing. It's crucial to stay agile, innovative, and forward-thinking to ensure your digital marketing strategy remains relevant and effective.

Navigating the Winds of Change

Dynamic Evolution

Recognize that the digital realm is a chameleon, undergoing perpetual transformations driven by technology, consumer behavior, and industry trends.

Evolving Algorithms

Stay attuned to the ever-changing algorithms of search engines and social media platforms, adjusting your strategies accordingly.

Agility in Action

Flexibility as a Virtue

Inscribe flexibility into your strategic blueprint, allowing for nimble adjustments to seize emerging opportunities or address challenges.

A/B Testing Philosophy

Embrace a culture of experimentation through A/B testing, leveraging data to make informed decisions that drive optimal results.

Integrating Cutting-Edge Technologies

AI-Driven Insights

Leverage the power of AI and machine learning to extract meaningful insights from data, steering your strategies with predictive precision.

Automation Efficacy

Integrate automation tools to streamline repetitive tasks, freeing your team to focus on strategic thinking and creative innovation.

Human-Centric Resonance

Empathetic Engagement

Cultivate deep connections by understanding and catering to your audience's aspirations, challenges, and emotional triggers.

Hyper-Personalization

Dive into the realm of hyper-personalization, crafting experiences so tailored that each interaction feels like a bespoke journey.

Sustainability and Ethical Practices

Green Values

Infuse eco-consciousness into your strategy, aligning with a growing consumer base that seeks brands with sustainability at their core.

Data Privacy Guardianship

Champion data privacy, ensuring transparent and ethical handling of user information to foster trust and loyalty.

Embracing Emerging Platforms

Innovative Platforms

Embrace emerging platforms that resonate with your audience, remaining open to disruption that may redefine your strategy.

Holistic Integration

Seamlessly weave new platforms into your existing ecosystem, creating a unified brand presence across diverse channels.

Investing in Knowledge

Team Empowerment

Nurture a culture of knowledge sharing and professional development, ensuring your team remains at the forefront of industry trends.

External Insight

Tap into external educational resources like industry conferences and thought leadership to gain fresh perspectives and insights.

Conclusion: Pioneering the Future Landscape

As you stand on the precipice of this profound chapter, equipped with wisdom, innovation, and a vision that transcends the horizon, remember that future-proofing your digital marketing strategy is a perpetual odyssey. Just as brands have forged paths of adaptability and creativity, your journey towards mastery is marked by the fusion of foresight and transformation. You are the architect of a future where your strategy stands as a testament to resilience, a resonating melody of relevance in the ever-shifting symphony of digital marketing. Your voyage is ongoing, painting a legacy where every engagement, every strategy, and every interaction echoes with your strategic prowess and visionary spirit.

5.11 Fostering Creativity and Innovation

In the kaleidoscopic world of digital marketing, where the canvas is ever-expanding and the palette constantly evolving, fostering creativity and innovation becomes the cornerstone of captivating crafting campaigns and strategies that captivate audiences and propel brands forward. In this chapter, we venture into the depths of artistic exploration, unearthing the methods to nurture creativity and inspire innovation in your digital marketing endeavors.

The Canvas of Creativity

Embracing Curiosity

Infuse curiosity into your approach, asking questions that challenge the status quo and provoke fresh perspectives.

Diverse Perspectives

Encourage a diverse team, as varied viewpoints spark a symphony of ideas that enrich the creative process.

Cultivating an Innovative Ecosystem

Risk as a Catalyst

Create a safe space for experimentation, allowing for calculated risks that often lead to groundbreaking breakthroughs.

Celebrate Failure

Shift the narrative around failure, viewing it as a steppingstone towards innovation rather than an impediment.

Nurturing a Creative Mindset

White Space for Ideas

Dedicate time for idea incubation, providing the mental 'white space' needed for creativity to flourish.

Cross-Disciplinary Learning

Encourage learning beyond the confines of digital marketing, drawing inspiration from diverse fields.

Inspiration in Data

Data-Powered Insights

Unearth insights from data analysis, using them as the foundation for innovative strategies that resonate.

Identifying Trends

Spot trends within data streams, acting as a compass guiding your strategy towards uncharted territories.

Collaborative Creativity

Brainstorming Brilliance

Organize collaborative brainstorming sessions, where ideas intermingle to form novel concepts.

Cross-Functional Fusion

Engage diverse teams across disciplines, combining talents for an alchemical blend of creativity.

The Role of Playfulness

Play as a Catalyst

Introduce playful elements into your strategy, as play can lead to unexpected, imaginative solutions.

Gamified Experiences

Infuse gamification into campaigns, inviting audience participation while sparking creativity.

Feedback Loop for Growth

Open Dialogue

Foster an environment where open discussions and feedback flourish, allowing for refinement and evolution.

Iterative Improvement

Embrace a cycle of continuous improvement, iteratively refining strategies based on feedback and results.

Technology as a Muse

Virtual Reality (VR) and Augmented Reality (AR)

Explore immersive experiences to engage users in entirely new ways.

Interactive Elements

Integrate interactive features into your content, encouraging audiences to engage on a deeper level.

Conclusion: Sculpting a Masterpiece of Innovation

As we draw the curtain on this chapter, remember that fostering creativity and innovation in your digital marketing endeavors is akin to nurturing a delicate seed that grows into a magnificent tree. Just as artists blend colors to evoke emotions, your role is to blend ideas, insights, and inspirations into campaigns that resonate with audiences. Your journey towards mastering creativity and innovation is an ever evolving one, marked by the symbiosis of exploration and execution. You're the curator of a digital masterpiece, where every campaign, every concept, and every innovation is a brushstroke that contributes to an ever-evolving canvas of digital marketing excellence—a canvas that dares to push boundaries, awaken curiosity, and sculpt narratives that etch themselves into the tapestry of brand resonance.

5.12 Sustaining Brand Relevance in the Everchanging Digital Landscape

Embracing the Currents of Change

Vigilant Awareness

Stay attuned to emerging trends, technologies, and shifts in consumer behavior to anticipate changes in the digital landscape.

Agile Adaptation

Develop a culture of adaptability that allows your brand to pivot swiftly, making the most of new opportunities and challenges.

Strategic Evolution

Data-Driven Insights

Harness the power of data analytics to understand shifts in audience preferences, allowing your strategies to evolve accordingly.

Scenario Planning

Envision potential scenarios and craft strategies for each, ensuring preparedness for unforeseen changes.

Continuous Relevance

Regularly audit and update your content to ensure it remains aligned with current trends, industry developments, and audience needs.

Evergreen Foundations

Build a repository of evergreen content that transcends trends, providing timeless value to your audience.

Personalized Engagement

Segmented Outreach

Utilize data segmentation to tailor your messaging to specific audience segments, delivering content that resonates on a personal level.

Dynamic Personalization

Explore real-time personalization, adapting your content based on user interactions to foster a deeply engaging experience.

Innovative Storytelling

Adaptive Narratives

Craft brand narratives that can adapt to changing contexts while remaining anchored to your core values and messaging.

Visual Storytelling

Harness the power of visual content to communicate your brand story in a compelling and easily digestible manner.

Cultivating User-Centricity

User Feedback Loop

Solicit feedback from your audience to understand their evolving needs and preferences, using this insight to shape your strategies.

Co-Creation

Involve your audience in content creation and decision-making, forging a sense of community and ownership.

Cross-Channel Resonance

Unified Messaging

Ensure a consistent brand message across all digital channels, fostering recognition and strengthening your brand identity.

Omnichannel Experience

Create a seamless user experience as your audience transitions between different channels, maintaining engagement and consistency.

Innovating Ahead of the Curve

Early Adoption

Embrace emerging technologies and platforms that resonate with your audience, positioning your brand as a pioneer in innovation.

Thought Leadership

Establish your brand as a thought leader by sharing insights, opinions, and predictions about the future of your industry.

Conclusion: Forging a Resilient Legacy

As this chapter draws to a close, you stand at the crossroads of a digital landscape that is both dynamic and promising. Sustaining brand relevance in this ever-changing environment requires a fusion of strategic foresight, creative adaptation, and an unwavering commitment to your brand's identity. Your journey towards mastering brand relevance is a testament to your brand's ability to evolve while staying true to its essence—a journey marked by the symphony of change and resonance. Just as brands have navigated the currents of digital evolution, your path towards mastery shapes a legacy where your brand remains an enduring beacon of relevance, inspiring audiences, and etching its mark in the ever-evolving narrative of the digital age.

5.13 The Future of Digital Marketing: Unifying Channels for Branding Success

As we gaze into the horizon of the digital landscape, it becomes evident that digital marketing's role in shaping the future is nothing short of pivotal. In this concluding chapter, we reflect on the profound importance of an integrated digital marketing strategy, where all channels collaborate harmoniously to create a symphony of brand resonance that echoes through time.

Digital Marketing's Future Significance

In the tapestry of the future, digital marketing is the thread that weaves brands into the fabric of consumers' lives. As technology continues to permeate every aspect of society, digital interactions become the lifeline through which brands can forge meaningful connections, capture attention, and inspire loyalty. The convergence of digital channels is set to amplify this impact, creating an ecosystem where brands can engage, educate, and entertain on a scale never imagined.

The Power of Unified Channels

The future is one of synergy—a harmonious collaboration of PPC, SEO, social media, and more. Unified channels present an opportunity for brands to amplify their voice, as each touchpoint reinforces the others, creating an immersive journey that captivates audiences across platforms. The resonance of a consistent message, tailored for each channel, creates a chorus that resonates deeply in the hearts of consumers, fostering trust and loyalty that transcends individual campaigns.

A Visionary Approach to Branding

In the future, branding will transcend the realm of logos and slogans, morphing into an immersive experience that transcends channels. A holistic digital marketing strategy embraces this evolution, crafting narratives that resonate with the essence of the brand while adapting to emerging trends and consumer preferences. This visionary approach ensures that brand identity remains both steadfast and adaptable, maintaining relevance as the digital landscape evolves.

Navigating the Uncharted Seas

The future holds uncharted waters, where technological advancements and changing consumer behaviors will continue to shape the digital sphere. By embracing an integrated approach, brands can navigate these waters with agility, adapting their strategies to stay aligned with the tides of change. The interplay of PPC's instantaneous visibility, SEO's organic credibility, and social media's engaging interaction creates a formidable vessel capable of conquering these evolving waters.

Conclusion: Pioneering a Future of Brand Resonance

As the final chapter of this journey unfolds, remember that the future of digital marketing is illuminated by the synergy of channels working harmoniously in pursuit of brand resonance. The horizon beckons with possibilities, and the visionary brands of tomorrow will stand as pioneers in this ever-evolving landscape. As technology, algorithms, and consumer behavior evolve, your journey towards mastering digital marketing will remain a testament to your ability to adapt, innovate, and create. Just as brands have navigated the tides of change, your path towards mastery forges a legacy where your brand resonates as a timeless force in the symphony of the digital age—a symphony where the notes of innovation, cohesion, and resonance blend into a crescendo of brand success.

Closing words

In the age of AI-driven search engines and Search Generative Experiences, the synergy between PPC, Content, SEO, and social media is nothing short of vital. It's not just important; it's the heartbeat of your digital presence.

Picture this: PPC, like a brilliant spotlight, grabs immediate attention, driving traffic and visibility. Content, the storyteller, weaves narratives that engage and resonate, creating a lasting impression. SEO, the strategist, ensures that you're found in the right place at the right time. And social media, the connector, fosters relationships, amplifying your message across a digital landscape.

But here's the magic: AI is the conductor of this symphony. It understands intent, context, and user behavior like never before. It anticipates needs, delivering hyper-relevant results. And it rewards those who collaborate, who merge their strengths into a harmonious crescendo of digital strategy.

This collaboration isn't just about visibility; it's about crafting unforgettable digital experiences. It's about understanding that your audience isn't a monolith; they're individuals with unique preferences and behaviors. AI empowers you to be where they are, when they want, and with what they desire.

Together, PPC, Content, SEO, and social media form an unbreakable alliance, guiding your brand through the labyrinth of the digital world. They are your torchbearers, illuminating the path towards customer engagement, brand loyalty, and digital success.

So, in this era of AI-driven transformation, remember this: Collaboration isn't just a choice; it's the key to thriving in a world where Search Generative Experiences rule. It's the fuel that propels your brand beyond mere visibility into the realm of genuine connection, relevance, and lasting impact. Embrace it, harness it, and let your digital journey be nothing short of extraordinary.

Thank you for taking the time to explore the pages of my book. Your interest and engagement mean the world to me. I hope you found it informative and inspiring. Your support is truly appreciated!

Cheers,

Veronika the digital Marketing hybrid Unicorn

Glossary

A/B testing a method in marketing research where variables in a control scenario are changed and the ensuing alternate strategies tested, to improve the effectiveness of the final marketing strategy.

above the fold the section of a Web page that is visible without scrolling.

ad blocking the blocking of Web advertisements, typically the image in graphical Web advertisements.

advertising network a network representing many Websites in selling advertising, allowing advertising buyers to reach broad audiences relatively easily through run-of-category and run-of-network buys.

ALT text HTML attribute that provides alternative text when non-textual elements, typically images, cannot be displayed.

B2B business that sells products or provides services to other businesses.

B2C business that sells products or provides services to the end-user consumers.

banner ad a graphical web advertising unit, typically measuring 468 pixels wide and 60 pixels tall (i.e., 468×60).

call to action (CTA) the part of a marketing message that attempts to persuade a person to perform a desired action.

CDN (content delivery system) a system of geographically distributed servers designed to accelerate the delivery of web pages and files by routing user requests to the server that's in the best position to serve them.

click-through rate (CTR) The average number of click-throughs per hundred ad impressions, expressed as a percentage.

contextual advertising a method of serving advertisements based on the content (i.e., overall context or theme) of a web page.

conversion rate (CR) the percentage of visitors who take a desired action.

cost per action (CPA) online advertising payment model in which payment is based solely on qualifying actions such as sales or registrations.

cost per click (CPC) the cost or cost-equivalent paid per click-through.

cost per lead (CPL) online advertising payment model in which payment is based on the number of qualifying leads generated.

CPM cost per thousand impressions.

customer acquisition cost the cost associated with acquiring a new customer.

eCPM effective cost per thousand impressions (technically, "effective cost per mille").

geo-targeting a method of detecting a website visitor's location to serve location-based content or advertisements.

HTML banner a banner ad using HTML elements, often including interactive forms instead of (or in addition to) standard graphical elements.

inbound marketing a marketing model whose sales performance relies on the initiative of its client base to find and purchase a product.

keyword a word used in performing a search.

keyword density keywords as a percentage of indexable text words.

keyword marketing putting your message in front of people who are searching using keywords and key phrases.

keyword research the search for keywords related to your website, and the analysis of which ones yield the highest return on investment (ROI).

keyword stuffing the excessive, unnatural use of keywords on a web page for search engine optimization purposes.

keywords tag META tag used to help define the primary keywords of a Web page.

link building the process of increasing the number of inbound links to a website in a way that will increase search engine rankings.

multivariate testing a method in marketing research where multiple variables in a control scenario are simultaneously changed and the ensuing alternate strategies tested, to improve the effectiveness of the final marketing strategy.

network effect the phenomenon whereby a service becomes more valuable as more people use it, thereby encouraging ever-increasing numbers of adopters.

organic search the unpaid entries in a search engine results page that were derived based on their contents' relevance to the keyword query.

pay per click (PPC) online advertising payment model in which payment is based solely on qualifying click-throughs.

pay per lead (PPL) online advertising payment model in which payment is based solely on qualifying leads.

pay per sale (PPS) online advertising payment model in which payment is based solely on qualifying sales.

return on investment (ROI) the ratio of profits (or losses) to the amount invested.

search engine a program that indexes documents, then attempts to match documents relevant to the users search requests.

search engine optimization (SEO) the process of choosing targeted keyword phrases related to a site and ensuring that the site places well when those keyword phrases are part of a Web search.

SERP shorthand for a page of search engine listings, typically the first page of organic results.

social networking the process of creating, building, and nurturing virtual communities and relationships between people online.

text ad advertisement using text-based hyperlinks.

title tag HTML tag used to define the text in the top line of a Web browser, also used by many search engines as the title of search listings.